BITTER GREETINGS

JEAN CARPER

☆

GROSSMAN PUBLISHERS

NEW YORK   1967

☆ ☆ ☆ # BITTER GREETINGS

The Scandal of the Military Draft

For THEA and JONATHAN

CONTENTS

BITTER GREETINGS

1 ☆ The Draft: Unquestioned

On the morning of July 13, 1863, a young Army officer was about to spin the lottery wheel in New York City's central draft office when a mob drove him off the platform, smashed the lottery wheel to bits with crowbars and burned the building to the ground. For three days, 10,000 citizens ran wildly through New York's streets in armed revolt against one of the most despised pieces of legislation in U.S. history: the National Conscription Act. The law, signed in desperation by Abraham Lincoln after two years of the Civil War, made all men eighteen through forty-five eligible for the draft by lottery.

But there was a way out for some. Legislators inserted into the law an odious clause to appease the wealthy northern gentlemen: Any man who paid $300 to the Provost Marshal, or who supplied a substitute, was exempt from the draft. Even moderately well-off shopkeepers might afford the bounty, but to laborers, earning $20 a week, it was a fortune.

This—our first federal draft law—was attacked throughout the country. One New York paper called it "tyranny of the worst sort, worthy of the most ruthless despot." Everywhere working men were hustled off to the battlefields leaving in their wake the bitter slogan: "It's the rich man's money and the poor man's blood."

New York City tolerated the draft lottery only one day before violence erupted. Spurred on by Confederate spies and a fury against the war to "free the niggers" who were taking white men's jobs, a crowd marched from Central Park down Broadway to the draft office, looting department stores and cutting telegraph wires along the way. Once destruction began, the crowd fed on it. They burned the state armory, and stormed Horace Greeley's *Tribune*. Men carried lead pipes, pick handles, knives, iron bars and stolen guns, and they used them. Women pulled officers off their horses and stoned them to death. Soldiers charged the mob with bayonets; and policemen rushed in with locust sticks, clubbing hundreds of men and women to death. Soldiers riding up Second Avenue at dusk on the second day of the riots saw the gutters filled with blood and the cobblestones littered with the dead and dying all the way from 21st to 33rd streets.

The mob's unleashed anger turned on the free Negroes living in the city. They set fire to the Colored Orphan Asylum on Fifth Avenue. Some of the children found refuge in a local police station. Others were caught and shot or beaten to death on a vacant lot through which they tried to escape. Rioters invaded the Negro ghettos and sent rows of shacks up in flames. Some men were seen throwing babies and women out of upper story windows into yards. In the haze of the steaming night, the mutilated bodies of several old Negroes could be seen dangling from lampposts.

New York City officials were stunned by the violence and seemed unable to control it. They even brought cannons into the streets and fired point blank into the rioters' ranks and against barricades made from wooden carts. The city council became so panicky that it called an emergency meeting and voted $2.5 million to pay for the exemption of future draftees who couldn't raise the $300. The law was promptly vetoed by the mayor after the uprising.

Finally, Secretary of War Edward Stanton promised to dispatch five regiments from Gettysburg to stop the riots. With the arrival of the soldiers, the crowds dispersed. On the fifth day, July 17, the streets were again orderly, although soldiers on horseback still patrolled the riot areas. That moment in history, now called simply "The Draft Riots of 1863," cost the lives of nearly 1,000 Americans.[1]

Today, protests against the draft have once again erupted with vehemence. But this time they are bloodless, confined to sit-ins, picketing, draft-card burning and verbal onslaughts. Our citizenry is not likely to set upon draft officials with clubs; we have grown accustomed to the draft's power to compel a man to military service. Our poor won't rise up against paid exemptions for the rich; today's draft law has no clause enabling men of means to buy their ways out. In fact, Congressmen in writing our law were so fearful of allowing class privileges that they specifically inserted a clause forbidding military substitutes or payments for exemptions.[2]

Yet, one can't help feeling that the present day is still troubled by the stirrings of a thousand gray ghosts. For the evils of our methods of forcing men to duty have not disappeared in the past hundred years. They have instead become more subtle and better hidden. In truth, the injustices and lies that men endure under our present draft system are in some ways similar and in many ways worse than those that led to the slaughter of 1,000 Americans a century ago.

Even a cursory look at the draft today reveals that class privilege did not die in the bloody streets of New York. If anything, it is operating more efficiently and viciously now than then. We no longer have a law that allows us to purchase exemptions by throwing down a fistful of dollars for Uncle Sam. We are more subtle than that. What father with cash cannot buy his son's way out of the war just as surely as the wealthy gentlemen of the

1860's did? As *Life* magazine observed in April, 1966: "Our system isn't much different from the one that prevailed in the North during the Civil War—just more expensive. In 1863, a draftee could hire a substitute for $300. Today his family does the same, in effect, by paying college bills that can run over $3,000 a year."

Nor need we dig far to discover other evidences of the miserable state of the draft. Why are there no Negroes on the draft boards of some southern states? And does it seem likely Negro boys are justly treated by boards whose members are leaders in the Ku Klux Klan? Why are low-paid clerks, instead of appointed officials, making life-and-death decisions of who shall get the greetings and who stay at home? Why should more boys in Michigan and Pennsylvania be drafted just because their draft boards are more efficient than those in Texas? Does it not seem ludicrous that we defer thousands of farm boys to produce food when the Department of Agriculture pays them not to produce food?

But still these sins, if we were categorizing them according to Dante, would be consigned to the outer circles. Deeper probing brings us to the very cellar of Selective Service's soul where the secrets of utmost significance are kept. Here we encounter a labyrinth of lies, and a corruption of American values.

• Why does Selective Service keep the nation in a panic over a manpower shortage when none exists? Why does it falsify figures to prove the "shortage?"

• Why does Selective Service cynically administer a college draft test when it has no intentions of using the results or of drafting college students?

• Why did the Pentagon suppress a study showing there was no need for a draft, and then reverse the conclusion before releasing it in June, 1966?

• By what right does Selective Service use the draft as an instrument of terror—to silence opposition to the Vietnam war?

• Is not the draft, in fact, one of our gravest threats to freedom because it is no longer used exclusively for military purposes but also as an insidious means of molding young men and society to conform to the ideals of aging generals?

Ironically, officials of the Selective Service in some of their press releases pat themselves on the back for never having suffered a scandal. They may be right if they define scandal as bribery, for if draft officials have traded their trust for profit—which indeed would be a great scandal—it has never reached the public's ear. Nevertheless, it would be a joke of the blackest kind for the American people to join in Selective Service's celebration of itself. For the truth is that the draft enjoys no *small* scandal. Its very existence, its operation, its Orwellian schemes and powers for controlling the nation's youth constitute a scandal of monstrous proportions. Contending there is no scandal in the draft is like saying there are no blackheads on that portrait of corruption rotting away in Dorian Gray's attic. For the draft, like the degenerate Dorian, suffers no small blemishes; it is corrupt of spirit all the way through.

Even the American public as a whole, although it cannot clearly see the body, can sense it rotting in the attic. A Gallup poll of June, 1966, showed that 38 per cent of the American people called the draft "unfair." And 43 per cent—barely four out of ten Americans—termed it "fair." These figures would not be so startling were they not *the lowest favorable vote that the American public ever registered on the operation of the draft during a war period.* Ordinarily, during wartime, Americans support the fairness of the draft by the overwhelming margin of nine to one.

Wartime has a way of exposing the ugly facts and shocking us into a realization of what is happening. Our boys are no longer going to foreign duty merely to stroll the hills of Bavaria or the streets of Tokyo. Some 9000 have already been killed in Vietnam. About one in five of our soldiers in Vietnam are draftees.[3]

These young men, though many do not protest their obligation, did not volunteer to end their existence in the Asian mud, nor spray flaming napalm on helpless Orientals. They are coerced into servitude by our Selective Service System. No man between eighteen and thirty-five is free of the draft's ever-watchful eye. An institution so powerful that it controls the lives of 33 million young men, the very heart of the nation, should be ever watched itself to make certain it is operating on the highest principles of justice and integrity. That no such claims can be made for Selective Service is becoming monstrously clear.

The draft system, of course, did not get into such a disgraceful state overnight. It grew and multiplied its ugly self through ten years of peacetime neglect when quotas were low and death remote. "Between 1953 and 1963," as the *Christian Science Monitor* observed, "the Selective Service was almost forgotten, as it bumped along lackadaisically and took in an annual low of 2900 men and a high of 6,000." So uninterested in the draft was the Senate that it renewed the Selective Service Act in 1963 after only ten minutes of debate. It has been fifteen years since Congress has given the Selective Service laundry a good airing, let alone a much-needed washing. The last time Congress seriously debated the draft law was in 1951 when the Selective Service Act of 1948 expired.

With the Vietnam war, criticism of draft policies has now reached fever pitch, especially among college students, educators and Congressmen. Much of the criticism is aimed at the war itself as well as the draft. But regardless of sentiment about Vietnam, a thorough investigation of the draft is long overdue.

It seems amazing, although not surprising considering the strength of pro-draft powers, that Selective Service, with complete power over a man's life and freedom, has never been subjected to an intensive public scrutiny. The opportunity for such probing usually comes every four years when the draft act expires. The current act is due for renewal by June 30, 1967. Some Congressmen hope to make extensive changes in the law at that time or, as Senator Edward Kennedy of Massachusetts suggests, the law might be extended for only six months to allow further study. Whether we will get in the near future a penetrating investigation into Selective Service depends in part on how cognizant the public is of the need and how vocal are its demands. Without public indignation, the prospect is rather bleak.

So far Congress has made but a farcical bow to public pressure by staging hearings on the draft before the House Armed Services Committee. The hearings began on June 22, 1966, and lasted six days. Although some Congressmen managed to get some disturbing facts on record, in general the sessions were given more to defending the draft than examining it.

Presiding over the hearings was chairman L. Mendel Rivers of South Carolina, who, it may be recalled, became so incensed over draft-card burners that he initiated a law making destruction of draft cards a federal offense punishable by five years in prison and a $10,000 fine. He refers to demonstrators against the draft and the war as "scum" and "vermin." Rivers is also a friend of Lieutenant General Lewis B. Hershey, director of the Selective Service System and chief witness at the hearings. Hershey at seventy-three is to Selective Service what J. Edgar Hoover is to the FBI. Because of their personal influence with Congressmen, both are known as the sacred cows of Capitol Hill, virtually beyond the reach of criticism.

For twenty-five years, under five Presidents and in three wars, General Hershey has hung on to his power through a humble, ingratiating, self-effacing relationship with Congress. Nowhere is he more beloved than in the House Armed Services Committee. As he entered the hearing room in June, the committee gave Hershey a resounding ovation, causing a Congressional aide to whisper, "Would you say the hearings are 'rigged?'" Chairman Rivers referred to Hershey, who was born on a farm in Indiana, as the "James Whitcomb Riley of Selective Service." When Hershey testified that he had indeed approved the reclassification of fifteen University of Michigan students 1-A for a sit-in at an

Ann Arbor draft board, Rivers looked down benevolently and
said in his southern drawl: "God bless you, you should have
done it. You should have done it."

Anyone who has ever seen General Hershey perform knows
that he is a master at hiding the facts or his ignorance of the
facts under a cloak of Hoosier folksiness and pretended candor.
It is refreshing at times to hear a government official admit he
doesn't have all the answers. But to a few serious Congressmen
trying to get at the truth, it was frustrating to hear Hershey ram-
ble, as he is wont to do, and often announce casually, when
pressed, that he did not carry around those kinds of facts. Typical was his response to Robert T. Stafford of Vermont, a
younger member of the committee who is not overawed by Hershey. Stafford asked: "Should the Selective Service make an
effort to assure that its regulations are interpreted identically
throughout the country?" Hershey answered: "Well, in the first
place, I would like to see your maples this fall, and the maple
syrup next spring, so I want to be as generous as I can. But in
the first place, I think you are dealing with human beings and I
think you are asking for somebody to create a machine that will
defeat human beings and I don't believe you have liberty and
uniformity at the same time. Now that is not a very good answer, but on the other hand, I have more confidence in those
people who live up in Vermont, for them to decide who ought to
go from up there than I have—and they have more compassion
even when they are a little granity—they have more compassion
than any of these machines have." [4] In this way were the attempts to get real answers thwarted.

Hershey testified for three consecutive days, unable to report
anything about the draft that needed change. The parade of wit-
nesses hostile to the draft was short indeed, and each one got
only fifteen minutes to state his objections. At the conclusion of
the hearings one Congressman commented in disgust that they
were only a token gesture "to take the heat off the issue for the
1966 Congressional elections." It appears unlikely that we will

ever get an honest, thorough investigation of the draft from this committee, dedicated as it is to its support of General Hershey and the Selective Service System.

Two days after the hearings, on July 2, President Johnson, eversensitive to criticism, made his placating gesture to America. He acknowledged good-humoredly that the draft system is a "crazy-quilt," and announced he had appointed a twenty-member citizen's commission to study the problem and recommend reforms. The commission is headed by Burke Marshall, former Assistant Attorney General under President Kennedy and now a vice-president of IBM. The commission includes several educators, among them Kingman Brewster, Jr., President of Yale, who has openly criticized draft policies.

No one can question the sincerity or capabilities of such a distinguished group, but one can question the President's motives in appointing them. Did President Johnson really hope the commission would dig up and expose to the public the grim truth about Selective Service? Or was the establishment of the advisory commission, which functions behind closed doors and makes polite recommendations, a means of keeping power in his own hands and warding off a full-dress Congressional investigation that might result in draft reforms not to the President's liking?

It would not be the first time the administration has used such strategy to kill a Congressional inquiry into the draft. To quote Robert Sherrill in *The Nation:* "In March and April of 1964, a great wave of enthusiasm was building up in Congress to really dig into the draft question and make some sense of it with a bipartisan Congressional committee. Both [Thomas B.] Curtis and former Senator Kenneth Keating had bills that looked promising.

"But only four days after Keating . . . introduced his draft review bill, President Johnson called a press conference and announced a 'comprehensive' review of the draft—to be conducted by the Department of Defense. He thus killed any chance Keating and Curtis might have had." [5] (As it turned out, the Department of Defense study, to have been published in 1965, is still top secret because it came up with the "wrong" conclusions. Only a summary was rushed into print in June 1966 after the conclusions had been changed to support the administration's war policies.)

If President Johnson was unwilling in 1964 to see the draft laid bare, it seems incredible that he would command such naked probing in 1966 when the draft was incalculably more vital to his war commitment. Some Congressmen think the commission's real purpose was to come up with enough Pentagon-inspired reforms, which could then be instituted by Executive Order and would forestall a Congressional investigation beyond the June 30, 1967 renewal deadline, so that we are forced to suffer another four years with a draft law carved out to suit the expediency of a President during wartime.

Selective Service is surrounded by intolerable secrecy, a secrecy that prohibits Americans from understanding and making judgments about the draft's existence and operation. The basic evil of the secrecy is that it allows the draft to continue for long periods virtually unquestioned; it also fosters thoughtless acceptance by the population.

We, unlike our forefathers, have come to accept the draft as part of American life. The draft has become an institution. We have forgotten that impressing men to serve in the military is a breach of individual freedom, justified by American tradition *only* when the country is in "clear and present danger." The draft forces a man to leave his family, his home, perhaps his children, his job; to give over the direction of his life to the state; to commit brutal acts against his fellow man which are normally repugnant to him, and to sacrifice his own life if need be. Should any nation ask this of its citizens without great soul-searching and except at times of grave threat to the country?

Yet we send conscripts to Vietnam without even a declaration of war. The draft, solely under the power of the President, has become a means of waging a war not even officially approved by

Congress. Moreover, only a few Congressmen, notably Senator Ernest Gruening of Alaska, have challenged the use of the draft to conduct such an undeclared war. Gruening insists that draftees should not be dispatched to Vietnam without Congressional approval.

Today, the draft is looked upon as permanent. A generation of men have grown up who cannot remember a time when the draft did not exist. In historical perspective, this situation is unparalleled and runs counter to our heritage. Americans usually associate peacetime conscription and large standing armies with the Prussian military character. Our own British heritage leads us to regard the draft as a temporary expedient for national survival. The draft was used as an emergency measure in the Civil War, World War I and World War II. After each conflict, it was allowed to die a natural death.

Only following World War II was the draft resurrected after a bitter debate. In 1948, military leaders convinced Congress that the Cold War was an emergency that demanded reinstatement of the draft. Any pretense of romance with Russia was over. The Berlin blockade was in progress. General Lucius D. Clay, American commander in Berlin, warned that war could break out with "dramatic suddenness."

President Harry S. Truman told the nation that armed forces were dwindling to dangerous lows and that we could not depend on voluntary enlistments alone. To counteract Russian "designs," Truman asked a joint session of Congress for a reinstatement of the draft and universal military training. Congress wisely rejected universal military training (UMT). But with tragic irresponsibility and lack of imagination they did not search for a modern method of manpower procurement. They turned to the easiest solution: They revived the old Selective Service System by passing the Selective Service Act of 1948.

Thus, on the heels of a Russian war-scare, we were given the peacetime draft that has persisted, with periodic extensions and revisions, for nineteen years. As we have seen, until now discussion of the draft has been so slight that the American people have not even had the opportunity to explore the possibility that the draft *not* be continued.

Failure to discuss the draft's possible demise is not accidental. The draft powers—the President, the military establishment, both Congressional Armed Services Committees and, of course, General Hershey—are dedicated to preserving the draft's existence in peace or war. Chairman Rivers opened the hearings of his committee in June, 1966 by making it clear that an attack on the draft's existence was not in order. He asserted that the figures dramatically illustrate "the absolute dependence of our Armed Forces on the assistance they get from the draft law. The facts appear abundantly clear—we do need a draft law for now and for the forseeable future." Defense Secretary Robert McNamara told a Congressional committee in February, 1966 that we could not expect an end to the draft in this decade.

Further, General Hershey resists any public probing that could damage the draft. He admitted to Congress that he might like some changes in the law, but was afraid to open the subject to public discussion for fear people would get ideas about extensive revisions that would be intolerable to him and the military establishment. "Let us . . . pray," he said, "that [this law] expires on a year that is not divisible by two." In other words, an election year, when the issue might be publicly debated.

Clearly, draft officials feel they do not dare risk a public airing of Selective Service. Americans given the truth would ask unacceptable questions, mainly the one draft proponents seek to keep buried: Why should we suffer a draft at all? A growing number of Congressmen who have privately studied the draft, including Representative Curtis and Senator Gaylord Nelson of Wisconsin, are convinced that a patchwork of reform on Selective Service is not enough. They favor abolishing Selective Service and establishing a voluntary army in its place. Prominent draft-critics, including Congressmen, government officials and educators came to a University of Chicago conference on the draft in December, 1966, prepared to reform the draft and, after intensive discussion, were so struck by the injustice of its existence and operation in a democracy that a majority signed a petition to abolish the draft.

There is no single, clear-cut reason why officials are unswervingly dedicated to preserving the draft. One immediate political motive, of course, is that the draft supplies an unlimited number of bodies to fight in Vietnam. Stripped of the draft and dependent on volunteers, the administration would probably be hampered in initiating and conducting land wars like Vietnam. As some University of Chicago conferees pointed out, without a draft, the use of Presidential prerogative to conduct war would be restricted.

The Pentagon says it needs a draft to summon up highly educated and skilled men, such as doctors and technicians, that the armed forces could not attract otherwise. General Hershey's desire to preserve the draft, and thus maintain his position and power, is understandable. Many Congressmen, namely Rivers' committee, have a paternal interest in the draft law, for they helped write it, and are convinced of its necessity.

Perhaps the most formidable and subtle force to keep the draft alive is psychological. We now have in power in this country a sizable group of men who paid their due to the military and their country in World War I and World War II. The legitimacy of the draft as an American institution is greatly strengthened by the attitudes of these men. In a paper submitted to the Chicago conference, Kenneth Boulding, professor of economics at the University of Michigan, pointed out why this is so. He said: "An institution [like the draft] which demands sacrifices can frequently create legitimacy for itself because of a strong tendency in human beings to justify to themselves sacrifices they have made. We cannot admit that sacrifices have been made in vain, for this would be too great a threat to our image of ourselves and our identity." [6]

This may help to explain why many men, principally older

military officers and veterans' groups, seek to preserve the draft with a zeal that can only be viewed as a display of vengeance toward youth. The attitude of the war-hardened soldier often is: "If I had to serve, why not you, too?" Often this vindictiveness is disguised as do-goodism. Some older men want to impress young men into service on the spurious justification that the Army is "good for a man's soul." Three powerful draft-proponents hold this view. L. Mendel Rivers, chairman of the House Armed Services Committee and Senator Richard Russell of Georgia, chairman of the Senate Armed Services Committee, which have jurisdiction over military manpower procurement, are staunch supporters of universal military training, which would draft virtually every young man for his own salvation. General Hershey, too, believes his mission will be complete when UMT is adopted and "local boards will be busier than ever, inducting everybody," and the military has set about reforming the character of all young men in America.

A realization of the strivings to preserve the draft, for whatever reason, is basic to any attempt to understand Selective Service. In the absence of this essential fact, the operations of the draft appear hopelessly confusing. For many of the draft's evils (inequities, student deferments and so on) are simply the result of trying to make the draft work, although it is an anachronistic wartime mechanism, completely unsuitable in times of peace or limited war, such as Vietnam. We must keep in mind during any evaluation of the draft the paradoxical truth that the draft does not exist to function as it does, but rather functions as it does, creating injustice, in order to survive.

How much longer must we tolerate attempts to hide the truth about Selective Service? When will Congress accept its responsibility for investigating the draft instead of abdicating that responsibility to Presidential commissions and biased Congressional committees? If we are ever to see the whole disgraceful portrait of Selective Service full-view, Congress should set up a joint, bipartisan, independent committee to conduct an inquiry into the draft. The committee could include members from Education and Labor Committees and the Armed Services Committees of both houses, the Senate Labor and Public Welfare Committee and other Congressmen appointed by the Speaker of the House and the President *pro tempore* of the Senate. Most important, the investigation should be conducted openly instead of behind closed doors.

There is little reason to think that we cannot obtain meaningful draft reform through an informed public and a determined Congress. For half a century, Congress was intimidated into inaction by the Detroit lobby; it was believed that safe automobile construction was an untouchable subject, that car manufacturers were too powerful to bring under Congressional criticism. Congress-induced changes in car design, achieved by legislation in 1966, are now history. The draft lobby, similarly, is big and powerful; but its nature is different, being composed of government officials, including the President himself. This fact, however, makes the issue all the more pertinent; for the Congress is charged by the Constitution to exercise a check on the executive and his appointed officials. If Congress takes this responsibility seriously, it can no longer permit Selective Service to go unexamined.

It is the purpose of this book to suggest avenues of investigation and to give readers an overall understanding of the injustices of the draft to enable them to demand such an investigation. This book is not void of judgments. On the other hand, the book does not presume to contain all the answers about Selective Service. Many questions will be raised to which answers can only be speculative. Nor does the book present a grand design for the construction of a new draft system on the wreckage of the old, although it will discuss proposals for change, including the feasibility of a voluntary army. The author does not want to be guilty, as so many Congressmen have been in the past, of closing the discussion to certain possibilities of change in compulsory military procurement before all the facts are in. However, it is probably inescapable that most readers, given the facts in this book, will reach the same conclusion as the author: That Selective Service is beyond repair, that it is a corrupt, unnecessary, basically terrifying mechanism that is antithetical to American freedom and should be abolished as quickly as possible.

2 ☆ The Waiting Game

> *"If the Selective Service System did not exist,
> it would be impossible to invent it."*
> —Daniel P. Moynihan, Director
> of the Joint Center for
> Urban Studies of MIT and Harvard

Once upon a time there was a mythical king who had so many soldiers he didn't know what to do. So he stewed and schemed and spent goodly amounts of time conceiving how he could conceal the terrible manpower surplus from his subjects. It would never do, he reasoned, to let it be known that the ancient custom, obliging every man to share service equally in the king's guard, had broken under the weight of an unimagined population boom.

Finally, the king called together the greatest brains from the kingdom's greatest universities, and for thirty days and thirty nights these learned men worked, and lo! one morning they saw the light and proclaimed their solution, based on a line from a long-forgotten epic poem: "They also serve who only stand and wait."

The king was delighted and had his scribes post a proclamation that henceforth most of the nation's men—in the vital interest of the country's health, welfare and safety—would serve by only standing and waiting. "Certain men are needed to stand and wait more than others," said the king. "And certain men are needed in the king's guards. Therefore, every man will be examined and classified to determine who shall serve by serving and who shall serve by only standing and waiting."

The learned men with the advice of the military put their wits to thinking up reasons why some men should serve best by only standing and waiting. One old general said he had noticed that all men born under the astrological sign of Gemini had a decided disinclination to fight on the battlefield. All men born from May 21 to June 21 were quickly classified G-I, as best left at home to serve.

Another general said he felt that men with hooked noses detracted from the appearance of soldiers on parade. So it was decreed that every man with a hooked nose be excluded from the army. But the degree of hook was a sticky problem. Scores of doctors had to be retained to measure the exact curvature, according to the degrees at which the tip of the nose reached its most prominent point.

After due consultation with drill sergeants, it was agreed that a man, with a 30-degree incline (designated H-3) to a 50-degree incline (H-5) might be considered fit soldiers only in all-out war. But those with noses ranging from 60 degrees through 80 degrees, H-6's, H-7's and H-8's, were too unsightly even for wartime, and a law was passed permanently excusing these men from his majesty's army. Strangely, hooked noses began showing up among the younger set, and it is said there was a thriving black market business in papier-mâché hooked noses that looked remarkably real.

The most successful ruse to relieve the embarrassing manpower surplus was to exclude those workers who were "vital to the nation's welfare." It started with the pomegranate pickers, this fruit being the favored one in the kingdom. Henceforth the king proclaimed that all pomegranate pickers would be classified PP-1. Pomegranate-picking quickly became the most honored profession in the land. Many young men who previously could not bear the sight of a pomegranate announced to their mothers that picking pomegranates was a lifetime dream. Nothing felt so good in the hand as a plump pomegranate, they declared.

Pomegranate farms grew up everywhere. Cartloads of rosy pomegranates on the way to market were seen constantly on the roads. Soon, the government had to build sheds in which to store the multitude of pomegranates. And the pomegranate farmers and truckers demanded that they be deferred too. So new classifications were devised—PF-1 and PT-1, which suited the king just fine.

Not long afterward, the obvious question arose: If pomegranate pickers, farmers and truckers are deferred, why not young men who are apprentices in pomegranate picking, farming and trucking? So new classifications were set up, dutifully recorded as PP-11, PF-11 and PT-11, for all boys attending pomegranate apprentice schools.

By following this pattern in all "critical" occupations, the king's advisers were happily able to draw up a list of 3,000 separate classifications of men exempt or deferred from military service, including the Masons (M-9) on religious grounds and the zither players of whom the king was so fond that he insisted they be classified from Z-1 through Z-9 depending upon their talent.

For years this system worked neatly with the populace as a whole content and none the wiser, until the king decided to enter a small scuffle with a neighboring kingdom of pygmies to the south. The king was certain he could dispose of his small enemy in short order, but the tiny pygmies proved wily and sneaky, and it took nine of the King's big stout men to subdue one pygmy.

As the king began to take a few more men from the AS-1

(available for service) pool, the country became more nervous. Some subjects thought the war was ludicrous, and didn't want to participate. Some PP-11's sat down in their pomegranate patches and refused to pick pomegranates to send to the troops. Even professors now opined that they could not justify philosophically why a boy's God-given talent at playing the zither should make him exempt from serving his country while boys with tin ears were being killed in South Pygmy Land.

The king and his generals were in a snit. They were outraged that the "standing and waiting" forces should show such ingratitude. "It is a royal privilege, and not a constitutional right," bellowed the king. He was hurt that the people were not enthusiastic about his war. "It's for the good of the natives," he said sadly. But mostly he was annoyed that his draft system was attracting so much critical attention, when he was so busy conducting a war. He promised to "study" the situation. Then he immediately undertook to frighten the subjects back into subservience. He first drafted the unruly pomegranate-picker apprentices who had opposed the war. He announced that the supply of AS-1's was dwindling rapidly and that he was considering drafting deferred men in 2,000 categories. He even scheduled a concert for zither players on the east lawn of the palace grounds to determine which, if needed, could be spared for the military, the least accomplished to be shipped out first.

Trumpeters proclaimed from the palace steps that virtually no one was exempt from military service at this critical time. And that is how it came to pass that millions of young men lived in fear of the draft while the king carried on his war and kept his power strong by pretending that his system was ultimately fair and put the burden of service on all men equally.

Any reader who has detected a marked similarity between the way the draft operates in this mythical land and in the United States is absolutely correct. Although the characters and motives are simplified, the essential plot is the same. Our Selective Service resorts to the same dishonest machinations as the mythical king. We are deluded to believe we suffer from a manpower shortage when in fact we are blessed or cursed, whichever way you view it, with a manpower surplus as never seen before in history. We, like the king, have so many soldiers we don't know what to do. And we, like him, must reach into the twilight of the ridiculous for schemes to cover up the surplus by pretending that millions of young men really do serve their country best by "only standing and waiting."

It is this surplus—not a deficit—of men and our frantic efforts to cope with it through a plethora of often-absurd deferments that is the real, largely unrecognized and little understood root of our ever-growing draft problems. As Congressman Henry S. Reuss of Wisconsin says: "In a nutshell, the trouble with the draft is that the military services require only about 400,000 men a year out of a pool of draft age men that now totals about 12 million."

Selective Service unavoidably is caught in the dilemma of a "peacetime" draft. The manpower supply is ever burgeoning, while military needs, in proportion to men available, are dwindling. In 1951, we had 8 million draftable Americans. By 1966 the number had risen to 18 million—an increase of 125 per cent in fifteen years. Today, we have about 1.8 million boys reaching age eighteen every year. The population explosion will push that figure up to 2 million by 1970 and 2.3 million by 1975. During peace, or small engagements like Vietnam, it is, has been and will continue to be preposterous to draft all men available into the armed forces. During the fifties and early sixties, the draft in some years called forth only 3,000 men. In some months the calls were zero. Today, even with the Vietnam buildup, as Congressmen Reuss pointed out, yearly draft quotas are expected to be little over 400,000. In fiscal 1966, for example, a "crisis year," only 340,000 men were inducted.

General Hershey likes to pretend—as justification for keeping the draft in existence—that the system upholds the so-called cherished ideal that every able-bodied young man should serve his country. "Selective Service," says Hershey, "spreads the duty and privilege of service throughout the population . . . to fulfill an obligation which is basic and universal." Our draft law, too, states this purpose of the draft: "In a free society, the obligations and privileges of serving in the armed forces . . . should be shared generally, in accordance with a system of selection which is fair and just."

Under the small requirements of the military, this concept of universality has been reduced to fiction. In 1951, only 70 per cent of the eligible young men were called into service. Today, only 46 per cent of all eligible men are donning an armed forces uniform. Our growing population will make the pretense of universality even more of a mockery. By 1974, if pre-Vietnam military strengths are resumed, only 34 per cent (little more than three out of ten Americans males) will ever be required to serve his country militarily.

Meanwhile, the draft swings heavy over every young man's head—only in make-believe. The mythology of equal obligation must be perpetuated by threat. But in truth, the draft summons up for the military only one man in every ten in the country. Figures of June, 1966, show that only 11 per cent of those serving came through Selective Service channels. All others were volunteers. Even under present Vietnam needs, "it doesn't take a mathematical genius," in the vernacular of General Hershey, to figure that we are drafting only *one man in forty* out of the nineteen to twenty-six age group.

The position of Selective Service becomes immediately ridiculous. They must select the few out of the millions and pretend to do it legitimately. They must pretend to make "wise" choices based solely on the needs of the country and the military. It is obvious that this abounding supply of men can't be "vital" one place or the other—either at home or on the battlefield. Yet, Selective Service, on one pretext or other, must insist that for every one man they induct, nine are better left at home to guard the hearth. To justify a "standing and waiting" force of 90 per cent of the available males, deferments are pushed beyond the credibility point. Excuses for deferments and exemptions are so flimsy that Congressman Seymour Halpern of New York calls the draft "a dangerous joke," and his colleague Del Clawson of California terms it "a laughing stock . . . harmful to our national security and the morale of our young men." Congressman Reuss points out the disconcerting fact that local boards that could manage to defer everybody would have to draft nobody. Says Reuss: "Selective Service regulations have been set up precisely to encourage local draft boards to grant deferments. Calls [for each board] are based on the number of men available after deferment. Thus, the more men who are deferred, the fewer calls the board will receive. Theoretically, a board which could defer everybody would receive no calls at all." [1]

We can smile over the silly antics of a monarch who would conjure up an elaborate structure of classifications in which to stow away young men to get them out of his hair. But our own Selective Service architects have a predilection for the same structures for the same purpose. In the words of *The Harvard Crimson,* the draft is like "some great Gothic cathedral that continues to grow and complicate itself." Our classification system, which has now expanded to eighteen letter-numbers, was not intended to be a whimsical hiding place for a surplus, but it has been magnificently corrupted to serve that need.

Every young man upon reaching age eighteen must, according to an act of Congress, register with his local Selective Service board. A few weeks later he is sent a classification questionnaire. From then on, indefinitely, he will be in a classification category ranging from 1-A (unconditionally available for service) to 1-C (member of the armed forces). (A complete list can be found in the Appendix.)

Through classifications, the boy's fate can be expertly manipulated according to the changing needs and moods of the administration, the Department of Defense and Selective Service. Local boards can shift men from one category to another, for example from 2-S (deferred for study) to 1-A to 1-C and eventually, unless he meets an untimely end at the hands of the military, a man will become 5-A (over-age). To soak up the surplus, draft powers can and do create new categories and reinterpret or rearrange old ones—especially 1-A.

Under the 1-A classification are six orders of call-up (priorities) which determine in orderly fashion which 1-A men will go first. The President establishes the priorities and can change them at will. At present, men are being called up from the 1-A pool in the following order: delinquents (those who fail to register for the draft or fail to perform other duties demanded by the draft law); volunteers (those who tire of waiting and ask to be drafted); single men and those married after August 26, 1965; those married before that date (Kennedy husbands); nonvolunteers twenty-six to thirty-five with extended liability; eighteen and a half- to nineteen-year-olds. Men nineteen to twenty-six are called, oldest first; those twenty-six and over are called up, youngest first.

The 1-A priorities were created purely to facilitate just and orderly choices. Today they are illegitimately used as deferment hiding places. Being in a low priority is the equivalent of being deferred. Many 1-A's remain comfortably untouched for years, some for the duration of their eligibility. When Hershey wanted to create a new deferment group—husbands—he had merely to persuade President Kennedy to put husbands in a low priority which would not be reached by most local boards.

Herein lies the central fact about our draft's corrupt state: Selective Service would like us to think that our intricate classification system operates to promote individual fairness, justice and the nation's welfare. Any small truth in this fades into insignificance beside the actual, bastardized use of classifications. Denuded of its glorious pretentions, our vast classification system—with its endless possibilities for deferment and exemption

—is little more than a ruse to cope with a monumental surplus, which, if loosed on the military, would overwhelm it.

The misuse of classifications is the source of our draft's sickness—its inequities, inconsistencies, absurdities, and ability to terrorize. The disease is the inevitable disease of our "peacetime" draft. By all evolutionary justice, Selective Service should have died twenty years ago with the end of World War II. But like other dying creatures that outlive their time, Selective Service attempted to acclimate itself to changing conditions by developing new functions and powers. Creatures trying to escape extinction are known to evolve many survival mechanisms—horns, legs where none existed, protective coloring, protruding eyes. Selective Service, in desperation to adapt to peacetime, took unto itself all varieties of functions, unrelated to its only true function of procuring men. It has therefore evolved into a dangerous, ridiculous looking creature—covered with horrible excrescences, the greatest of which is the vast system of deferments with which it tries to justify and prolong its existence, and with which it spreads injustice and fear.

Only since World War II has the deferment system been perverted from a method of preserving the nation to a means of preserving the draft. The original intent of deferments, since Revolutionary War days when state militias exempted iron workers and surgeons, has been to keep men where they could best serve a *war* effort. When a nation is mobilized for all-out war, deferments are a logical outgrowth of self-preservation. It is national suicide to indiscriminately send bomber designers, nuclear physicists and munitions experts off rifle-slinging in the ranks of the military. In war, the only basis for deferment is whether a man's skills for saving the country are best used in battle or at home. In World War II, this meaning of deferments was clearly applied. Some 125,000 college students a year were deferred, not because they were superior beings or even indispensable to post-war recuperation. A 1942 memorandum instructed boards to defer only college students who were "necessary men, in training and preparation for any industry, business, employment, agricultural pursuit, governmental service or other service or endeavor, the maintenance of which is *essential to the support of the war effort.*" [2]

In a great conflict like World War II, where a true manpower shortage exists and every man, civilian or soldier, counts toward the military effort, Selective Service can speed along with single-minded purpose: winning the war. Deferments are an integral part of that purpose. In peacetime or limited war, like Vietnam, deferments are robbed of their *raison d'être* and become a mockery. It can no longer be argued that the nation's survival depends on the utilization of every man either at home or on the battlefield. Only a few men are essential on either front. Once used legitimately to cope with a severe manpower shortage, deferments are then grotesquely twisted to deal with a gigantic manpower surplus. The draft, deprived of its function of procuring and distributing the nation's men, is obsolete, useless and by its very nature destined to be absurd and unjust.

The integrity of Selective Service crumbled with the reinstatement of the draft in 1948. Congress may not have perceived the grave implications nor difficulties of reviving Selective Service. But the problems of peacetime mobilization became immediately apparent to General Hershey and his staff. They were charged with drafting 250,000 men in fiscal year 1949 out of a manpower pool of 7.9 million. As General Hershey noted, they had to be more "selective" than during the war when 16.5 million men were taken into the armed forces. To lend any semblance of justice to their choices, they had to first shunt most of the male population off into acceptable deferment categories. There were not enough deferment categories to soak up the surplus. So Selective Service, with the aid of the Defense Department and other national leaders, set about creating them, and continues to do so when the supply becomes unmanageable.

With the ink hardly dry on the draft act, General Hershey called a meeting for November 4, 1948, to work out ways the rejuvenated Selective Service could grant liberal deferments to college students. In retrospect, this is one of the most significant moves in the history of the draft. No longer could the draft maintain the necessity argument that these boys should be left on campus because they were vital to the war effort, for of course there was no war. With admirable sleight of hand that went virtually unnoticed, Selective Service altered the historic meaning of deferments for the sake of convenience. Contribution to the war effort was no longer the sole criterion for deferment. General Hershey, on the advice of twenty-seven nationally respected educators, scientists and executives, called the Scientific Advisory Committees, announced that students should be deferred simply because they were more valuable than other boys to the future "health, safety and interest of the nation." It was a monumental social judgment to make and to implement. Unfortunately, this interpretation of deferment is permissible under the letter of the law, although it undoubtedly was not the intent of the law. (The language is a carry-over from the 1940 Selective Service Act, which was loosely phrased because we were still technically at peace, although the clear intent of the law was to prepare for war that had already broken out in Europe.)[3]

Nevertheless, the law, intentionally or not, gave Hershey license to initiate a sweeping new deferment policy and, more important, and almost incredible in its ramifications, allowed him to make a momentous leap from mere jurisdiction over defense manpower to control over civilian manpower in time of peace. Using the draft to promote the nation's "health, safety and interest" in peacetime has unlimited possibilities, and Hershey has made use of them, as we shall see in a later chapter. In essence, the old soldier hoisted onto his Hoosier shoulders some weighty problems that have plagued the world's philosophers for centuries; among others, How shall society be organized? Hershey was no longer just master of our fate in defense matters; he was elevated to the role of omniscient organizer of society, with the remarkable presumption to know what is best for us all—in war or peace. That the draft's authority slipped over from war-time procurement to an area where it has no moral right to be—regulating manpower for peacetime—without a whimper of protest, and in fact with the thoughtless complicity of our educators, seems astounding today. Given the climate of 1948—the growing fear of Russia, rearmament, the predictions that atomic war was imminent, and the fascination with the notion of scientists as our future salvation—the draft's expansion of power is more understandable.

Selective Service did not have to defend its vast student deferment policy vigorously at first, although when pressed during the Korean hostilities, it tried valiantly to cover up its prime motive with a mountain of irrelevant arguments, the main one being that the future military posture of America depended on scientists being trained in universities. (Actually, boys in all fields of study were being deferred.) But during a radio discussion in April, 1951, Brigadier General Louis H. Renfrow, then deputy director of Selective Service, inadvertently told the true reason behind student deferments when he said: "Neither must we overlook the fact that we cannot accommodate in the military forces at the present time all of the men who are liable for active duty." [4] His was an understatement. Drafting these 700,000 college boys then deferred would have swamped the military ship.

As might be expected, going to college became as popular as pomegranate picking or zither playing in our mythical kingdom. In the spring of 1951, college presidents were gloomily predicting a 50 to 75 per cent drop in enrollment. This was before the college deferment, replete with deferment test, had been instituted full force. By fall, however, college registrations were higher than expected nearly everywhere and were running within 10 per cent of the previous year. This led *U.S. News and World Report* magazine to proclaim: "Draft Helps Fill Colleges," which "indicates that the controversial student deferment plan is working." Indeed, the "deal between the educators and Selective Service," as Congressman Curtis calls it, did seem to work well.

Selective Service was disposing of thousands of unwanted men by pushing them through the portals of floundering colleges.

Between 1951 and 1965, college enrollment more than doubled by rising from 2.2 million to 5.6 million, and the number of deferred college students increased nearly 250 per cent to 1.7 million in 1965. Although the entire influx of college students can be attributed to the draft, educators agree that it exercises considerable influence. Paul Goodman, social critic and well-known author of such books as *Growing Up Absurd,* in the fall of 1966 told freshmen at Rutgers University that one of the three main reasons for going to college was to avoid the draft.

In 1962, General Hershey's office, realizing it was about to be struck by a tidal wave of young men born during the postwar baby boom, devised, in conjunction with the Pentagon, an ingenious new classification, called 1-Y. The meaning of the classification is wonderfully vague, affording an expanding scale of interpretations of why a man should be in deferment limbo, somewhere between 4-F and 1-A. A man in 1-Y is not too objectionable for war, not perfect enough for 1-A in peacetime, but acceptable in an emergency.

At least within the context of the "new XYZ evaluation program" which spawned the classification, the term means precisely as it says—1-Y. Selective Service tells us that under the new system, the symbols X, Y and Z denote the degrees of qualification of a registrant. X means qualified unconditionally, Y means qualified in an emergency or all-out war, Z means unqualified. Thus, the "XYZ evaluation" of four registrants might be:

Physical (medical)	Mental	Moral
X	X	X
X	Y	X
Y	Z	Y
Z	X	Z

A boy who gets three X's is in; a boy with one Z is definitely out, and a boy with one Y is maybe.

Although we might think it ludicrous to exclude a man because the shape of his nose did not suit the military's fancy, the justification for deferring 1-Y's is on the same level and for the same basic reason. The 1-Y's have only minor imperfections that do not conform to the military's image of itself, which grows more esoteric as the manpower supply increases. In this nonmythical kingdom of the United States, it is not H-3 through H-6 who are in the military twilight zone. But it is BB-1 (beginning bunion); TT-1 (too thin); AM-2 (asthma maybe) and HS-3 (hypertension sometimes). These are not fictitious reasons. Men have been declared 1-Y for all of the above defects.

It's hardly surprising that the 1-Y classification has netted us some interesting exemptions, such as Cassius Clay, heavyweight boxing champion of the world, who nevertheless is deemed too dumb to fight for his country except in dire emergency.* No outstanding 1-Y's in the moral category have come to public attention, unfortunately, for military examiners must be making some imaginative decisions in this area. Deciding who is just a bit too depraved for peace, but not too depraved for war, must be a challenging task.

In 1963, the 1-A manpower pool once again became embarrassingly large and cumbersome to manage. It held 1.7 million men; yet draft quotas were running only 7,000 monthly. In September, 1963, President John F. Kennedy, at the urging of General Hershey, announced that married men henceforth would be put in a low priority, unreachable by the current needs of draft boards. In one swoop, 340,000 husbands were virtually removed from the manpower pool. The public excuse was that married men had more right to an uninterrupted life than single men and therefore should be deferred.

---

* Clay, under reduced standards accepting high school graduates who scored low on the mental test, was reclassified 1-A, and ultimately appealed for a 4-D classification as a Black Muslim minister.

The real purpose of the deferment of married men is indisputable. A high-ranking Army officer who was on the scene when General Hershey persuaded President Kennedy of the action told me: "The Selective Service System is desperate to hide the surplus of men and had to find something to justify taking only the few needed men, so they shunted the married off into a deferment category. The only reason Hershey talked Kennedy into deferring husbands was to cut down the manpower pool. If Hershey doesn't hide the surplus, it will appear gargantuan, and he is afraid more people will begin to say 'We don't need a draft.' "

Few citizens had the knowledge to question the exemption's true purpose or basic illegality. Even so, is it in the nature of husbands on the eve of freedom to beware a government bearing gifts? It was barely noted that the exemption of husbands had been accomplished surreptitiously by an administrative juggling of the 1-A priorities and, although not technically illegal, was contrary to the Selective Service Act. Under section 6(h) of the law, Congress empowered the President to defer men with dependents, defining dependents as "not wives alone, except in extreme hardship." As Congressman Fred Schwengel of Iowa points out, "Clearly Congress had no intention to exempt married men," and "to discriminate against bachelorhood." But in the frantic rush to conceal the surplus and preserve the draft, attention to such minor moralities vanish.

Although it was September, young men's thoughts turned curiously toward marriage. Col. Harry O. Smith, director of the draft in Georgia reported: "In one week we had forty-six men who had been ordered to report for induction suddenly get married." From 1962 to 1965, the number of marriages, which had been on a steady keel for several years, went up 15 per cent, and the marriage rate in relation to total population increased by 8 per cent. Creating social evils is not one of the draft's stated functions, but is surely one of the effects. While national leaders struggle to control a population explosion and discourage early, hasty marriages, which often end in divorce and societal disruption, General Hershey blithely counteracts their efforts with one whimsical draft edict.*

With each year, as the male population grew, so grew Selective Service's determination to bless young men with deferments. In 1965, they granted 19,000 deferments to keep men on the farms to grow food. That was the same year the Department of Agriculture paid out $3.3 billion in price supports and subsidies to farmers not to grow food and spent nearly $300 million to carry away tons of unneeded food.

Deferments of men in critical occupations increased steadily. In 1956, 29,000 men were excused from the military because they were in critical jobs on the home front. The number rose to 53,000 in 1959; 111,000 in 1962; and 204,000 in 1966. In ten years, the need for essential workers in the nation's defense, according to Selective Service, went up 700 per cent, although only in the last two years have we been in military conflict.

Before Vietnam, to obtain deferment, it was no longer necessary to be a bona fide student (just take a two-hour night course) nor a drug addict (just say you were one). "Soon they'll be exempting boys with red hair," remarked a professor. Perhaps the culmination of Selective Service's desperation to stem the flow of manpower is found in the deferment of actor George Hamilton by a New York City draft board. Hamilton has (and has had since age eighteen) a hardship, 3-A deferment because in the words of syndicated columnist Sheilah Graham, he is "the sole support of his fashionable, multi-married mother, Anne Potter Hamilton Hunt Spaulding and two quite grown-up brothers— Dave and Bill—one of whom works as an agent with McCann-Erickson and the other who is an interior decorator, responsible for gussying up George's $250,000, thirty-nine-room mansion in

* In 1965, President Johnson put men married after August 26 of that year back on a priority par with single men. "Kennedy husbands" are still drafted after "Johnson husbands" which once again only illustrates the inconsistent and arbitrary nature of deferments.

Beverly Hills, called the Pickfair estate . . . one of the Holly-wood showcase mansions built by Douglas Fairbanks and Mary Pickford." During the past nine years, Hamilton has reportedly averaged $150,000 income a year and in 1966 was receiving about $125,000 per picture. His "hardship" classification was reviewed in June, 1966 and was renewed. When questioned about Hamilton's deferment by Yale students, General Hershey replied, "I don't read much about the movie business so I didn't even know he was alive till this summer."

Hamilton professes irritation over the publicity of his draft status and says he will go to Vietnam if called. Part of Hamilton's dilemma is actor's vanity. Although the fact does not lessen the absurdity of his thirteen-year-long deferment, records reportedly show he is not twenty-seven as he claimed in 1966, but thirty-one, and has been over the normal draft age of twenty-six for the last four years.[5]

With the Vietnam crisis and the rising draft calls, deferments were tightened somewhat, although not nearly so much as most people assume, and not because of any serious manpower squeeze. By pulling in the rein on deferments, and pretending to, Selective Service tries to "equalize" and hide the inequities of the system and minimize criticism of the draft and the Vietnamese war. In reality, Selective Service is fighting the manpower bulge as much as ever.

At present we have 18.5 million men of suitable age for military service. Of these nearly 2.5 million (about 14 per cent) are veterans who have already served. Three and a third million are now in the armed forces, including about 550,000 draftees. Another 1,200,000 are in the reserves, including Reserve Officers Training Corps (ROTC) and the National Guard. That leaves nearly 12 million eligible for service. The Department of Defense estimated in the fall of 1966 that calls for the following months should run not more than 35,000. In November, 1966, McNamara amended that figure, reducing the prediction to 25,000 a month. It probably will be even slightly lower.

Projected for the year, the number of men drafted may range from 200,000 to 420,000, a figure that is insignificant beside the supply.

With 12 million men liable for duty and only half a million men liable for call in a year, we can appreciate the magnitude of Selective Service's problem. It is, in effect, stuck with an excess of 11.5 million men for 1967. Actually, it solves part of the surfeit problem by keeping a million men, about 8 per cent of the total supply of nineteen to twenty-six-year-olds, in the 1-A pool, thus immediately available for induction. Still, Selective Service must keep 11 million men, 92 per cent, properly pigeon-holed, out of public view so they can ship the unfortunate half-million off to boot camp—and possibly Vietnam—as quietly as possible.

During peace, the deferment process is little examined. The nation is not overly fastidious in demanding reasons behind "selections." Most of us are willing to avert our eyes, thankful that the draft is leaving so many young men alone. Indulging Selective Service in its deferment game seems relatively harmless, even beneficial to most. During wartime, however, the conscience begins to hurt. It is increasingly difficult to overlook the arbitrary reasons why 11 million men should "stand and wait" in safety while another group of half a million is sent off to possible death. General Hershey's answer that "after all, all life is a risk," does not seem adequate.

The nation, as demonstrated by polls, is angry about the draft. Unfortunately, the anger is often misplaced through lack of understanding. Much of it focuses on the so-called draft dodger—the "scum and vermin," as the chairman of the House Armed Services Committee labels them—rather than on the corruption of a system that fosters, even begs for evasion of service in order to survive. When officials set up make-believe, cynical ways to keep men out of the overflowing 1-A pool, why should we be surprised when young men mockingly accept the invitation, by going to graduate school, by entering professions they care little about and covering their arms with pin pricks to feign drug-addiction? Senator Gaylord Nelson has said: "We are stuck with a system which supplies far more men than we can use, so . . . we corrupt the system by providing more and more ways to avoid the draft. We actually encourage our young men to seek ways to avoid service." [6]

"A cynical avoidance of service," says one educator, "is consistent with the rules of the deferment game." Draft officials behave much like the old-time movie heroine, who, while being ravaged by the hero, winks knowingly at the audience.

Selective Service, as we know it, is a wartime mechanism that can function honestly only in total mobilization when all men are necessary. When misused to deal with peacetime needs or small conflicts like Vietnam it loses the core of its integrity. It no longer operates to dispense pure justice, but strives to dispose of the surplus of men in the most convenient, self-serving manner. We can contemplate the depth of its corruption when we consider that a system set up exclusively to procure men for the military now expends nearly all its efforts devising ways to keep men home. As long as Selective Service is allowed to bastardize deferments and exemptions in its pitiable struggle to cope with the surplus and maintain its existence, there can be no happy ending to the situation.

3 ☆ The Mythical Manpower Shortage

In July, 1965, the nation was officially notified by President Johnson of the escalation of the Vietnam war. The President announced that the build-up of troops would necessitate a doubling of draft calls to 35,000 by the following October. At first, Selective Service calmly went about its task of calling up the extra men. In November, General Hershey's office was assuring us there was no manpower crisis, and decrying the "panicky speculation" which had been set off by news reports of the rising draft quotas.

But by January, 1966, General Hershey had done an about-face. He now declared that we were in the midst of a manpower crisis so severe that we might have to dip into college students, comb through the 1-Y's and overturn every deferment rock in a desperate search for potential soldiers. "Perhaps even turn to the reserve units who aren't doing anything," he said.

One week he promised he would not consider reviving the controversial college deferment test; the next week he said it was imperative. He began rounding up state draft directors into three regional meetings to discuss ways to meet the worsening manpower shortage. Hershey inexplicably mentioned high monthly draft calls of 50,000 to 80,000, a mysterious figure which could not be verified by the Pentagon, and had not been mentioned by anyone else in authority. Later, he conceded it was not a valid figure, and that he had seriously anticipated calls of only 40,000 —which, as it turned out, was still too high. It should be said that anyone who tries to follow the changing pronouncements of General Hershey will have a vertiginous time of it. Consistency, to rephrase Emerson, is not a hobgoblin of the old general's mind.

Throughout the spring, Hershey's office kept college students in a state of anxiety. The climax came in May and June of 1966 when in four days, 750,000 boys took the draft deferment test in the belief it would influence their draft status. Never before had so many college boys been stampeded by fear of the General's ominous shadow. The number who turned out to take the test equalled all those who had taken the previous twenty-eight tests given over the past fifteen years.

After the furor over the tests died down, Secretary of Defense Robert McNamara, in cooperation with Selective Service, put a chill into the hearts of the 1-Y's. In late August, he disclosed that he would lower the physical and mental standards to draft 40,000 1-Y's before June, 1967, and 100,000 the following year. Local boards were kept busy for weeks answering the alarmed calls from 1-Y's worried about their status.

In October, Selective Service let it leak out via a memorandum to state directors that not even the men between twenty-six and thirty-five—who thought they had reached the over-age draft Nirvana—were safe. Those previously deferred were ordered in for physical examination. On October 4, 1966, the *Chicago Tribune* ran a banner headline: "Older Men Facing Draft," followed by the subhead: "70,000 in 26 to 35 category affected." A recruiting sergeant said the news produced a landslide of enlistees who were trying to avoid the draft. One thirty-year-old man who had received a college deferment but had subsequently been classified 1-Y because of high blood-pressure, talked with me for forty-five minutes in a state of nervous upset. Although I pointed out that his chances of being drafted were extremely remote, he was not reassured. His solution was to stop taking the pills that kept his blood pressure down.

One could hardly be blamed for thinking we were struggling with a critical manpower shortage. From all appearances, we were reduced to drafting college students and 1-Y's and now reaching to the bottom of the manpower barrel for thirty-four-year-olds in fashion reminiscent of World War II.

A closer look, however, reveals that the draft was taking very few of these men. During 1966, the draft only *directly* threatened some 100,000 deferred men with imminent induction. But by casting its eye back and forth over the entire population of college students, 1-Y's and over-twenty-six-year-olds, it indirectly struck fear of the draft into over four million deferred American males and their families, plus one million 1-A's who knew they would be called up first.

As expected, many did not wait to receive their "Greetings." They enlisted. Enlistments in the Army, Navy and Air Force went up from 350,000 in fiscal 1965 to 600,000 in fiscal 1966 —an increment of 70 per cent. The draft's familiar scare techniques were working. The so-called manpower shortage, coupled with increased draft calls and threats to the deferred, was having an effect.

It is appropriate at this point to inquire into the legitimacy of General Hershey's claim of a manpower shortage. Was our lack of men in the 1-A pool so severe that it warranted drafting college students and other deferred men? Or was the crisis phony?

Only five months earlier, Norman S. Paul, then assistant secretary of defense for manpower, had shrugged off any suggestion that we were heading for a manpower shortage. When asked by a *U.S. News & World Report* interviewer in August, 1965, if the pool of 1-A's was large enough to meet needs, Paul replied: "Oh yes, more than enough to meet any contingency we can foresee." He said emphatically that we could go ahead with the Vietnam build-up without altering any deferments, including those for students.

In January, 1966, Frank Mott, who keeps track of military manpower for the Labor Department's Office of Manpower, Automation and Training, was quoted in the *New York Herald Tribune* as saying that he could see no justification for Hershey's frantic search for 1-A's. "So far as we can judge, there should be no problem meeting draft needs, even with the increased call."

In February, 1966, the Subcommittee on Education of the House Committee on Education and Labor held hearings on manpower problems relative to education.[1] During the testimony, Congressman Ogden R. Reid of New York, on behalf of a group of twenty-five liberal Republican Congressmen known as the Wednesday Club, asked General Hershey to explain how there could possibly be a manpower shortage that would warrant drafting college students. General Hershey agreed to supply statistical proof justifying his prediction of the shortage. According to one Wednesday Club member, this "proof" did not exist at the time Hershey offered it, and it was drummed up, apparently with great haste, to justify a nonexistent shortage. The first copy of the report that came to the Congressmen's office contained an arithmetical error of 100,000 men. (In adding four numbers, the Selective Service statistician came to a total of 388,836 instead of the correct figure of 288,-836. This mistake seems to confirm the suspicion that the report was drawn up after-the-fact specifically to "prove" a deficit to the Congressional Committee; it seems unlikely it could have existed for two months in Selective Service offices with such an obvious error undetected.)

After the error was pointed out to draft officials and corrected, Selective Service then contended that by June 30 we would have *minus* 5,207 men available and qualified in the 1-A pool unless we reclassified some deferred men, including college students. Admittedly, for Selective Service, which has rarely failed to deliver the ordered number of soldiers, it would be an ignominious state of affairs to arrive at June 30 with 5,207 men in the red. But the doleful prediction of the draft's statisticians had no basis in fact. One might say it was preposterous, even inexcusable, considering that General Hershey used this fictitious report to stir up a cauldron of draft fears. The report contained several inaccuracies and one notable omission.

The report was predicated on the assumption that draft calls would be 40,000 a month for the coming five months—February through June. In only one of these months did the calls reach 40,000. In February, calls were 25,400; March, 22,400; April, 19,200; May, 40,600 and June, 18,500. Actual calls for the five-month period were only 64 per cent as high as estimated. It is true that Hershey's office could not predict with precision the draft calls five months in advance. However, the Department of Defense determines the exact number of draftees needed and then forwards that figure to Selective Service, which then issues draft calls. Hershey's office is notified of draft calls by the Department of Defense two months in advance. In February, when he made his report to the Congressional Committee, quoting the 40,000 figure, Hershey had already issued draft calls for February and March. These alone precluded any possibility of a 5,207 man deficit.

Not only did Hershey fail to correct his mistake, he repeated and compounded it. In reply to a request from Illinois Senator Everett M. Dirksen for information on manpower needs, Hershey, in a memo dated March 2, 1966, reasserted that we faced a dire manpower crisis by June. Dirksen inserted the information into the Congressional Record, unfortunately giving it more credence and circulation among congressmen. However, by the time Hershey wrote Dirksen, the General had issued draft calls for April and for May. These lower draft calls would have affected the report's validity, if indeed it ever had any.

Detecting the report's more serious and subtle errors requires the knowledge of someone familiar with the procedures used in figuring manpower needs. To confirm the Selective Service report's inaccuracy, I enlisted the help of a military manpower expert at the U.S. Department of Labor, who prefers to remain unnamed in print. Contradicting General Hershey, even in the interests of accuracy, is not always viewed by the Administration as a public service.

In general, my authority pointed out that the Selective Service report built its case by 1) using conservative estimates and, 2) tending to leave important things unsaid. Selective Service correctly assumed that 150,000 nineteen-year-olds would enter the 1-A pool each month. But draft statisticians estimated that 130,000 of these youngsters would end up elsewhere than in the 1-A pool. For example, some would enlist prior to their nineteenth birthdays; some would be deferred to finish high school or go to college; some would become fathers or hardship cases; some would be disqualified. Thus, Selective Service figured that only 13 per cent, or 20,000 of the new nineteen-year-olds would find their way into the 1-A pool each month. "This is very conservative," said the Labor Department authority. "We would be more likely to estimate that 30,000 of these nineteen-year-olds —or 20 per cent—would end up in the 1-A pool per month." Labor Department figuring thus would have automatically put 10,000 more new nineteen-year-olds per month—or 50,000 more men in the five-month period covered by the report—into the 1-A pool.

The Selective Service report inexplicably does not take into account that men from other age groups besides the nineteen-year-olds will also be coming into the 1-A pool. As General Hershey himself has pointed out, the 1-A pool is not still water; it is more like a river with depths and currents. Men are always flowing in and out. It is to be assumed that during a five-month period, many men will be transferred from deferred status to 1-A status. For example, Selective Service made no allowances for the influx of 1-Y's who became 1-A's under reduced mental standards. Nor did Selective Service consider that a number of college students who were not 1-A in January would be 1-A in June when they flunked out or dropped out of college. "As Selective Service knows," to quote my authority, "June is a big month when they get a lot of new men in the 1-A pool."

All of the above are small errors in calculation; but when you are dealing with large numbers, they can be multiplied into a significant sum. However, after carefully studying the report, the Labor Department expert determined that its conclusion was most seriously prejudiced by a peculiar omission. Selective Service chose to ignore the existence of some 340,000 1-A men caught in what is known as the "pipeline." These were men who, for some reason, were not immediately available for induction or examination. It is assumed that the "limbo" status of the majority of those men will be resolved, and that many will be draftable.

But in the report to Congress purporting to prove the manpower shortage, Selective Service included only 279,676 1-A men as being in the pipeline—"not available because ordered for examination." In their own files, and generally available, Selective Service has another report, dated January 31, 1966, that correctly shows 621,505 men in the pipeline—"not immediately available for induction or examination." What became of the 341,829 missing 1-A's? Apparently, a funny thing happened to Selective Service officials on their way to Congress. In transferring the figures from their own report to the one intended for Congress, they conveniently lost some 340,000 men.

The most telling proof of the magnitude of the report's incredible inaccuracy was the size of our 1-A pool when June 30 did arrive. It did not bring the deficit doomsday so fearfully foretold. By applying the same figuring techniques used by Selective Service in its prediction, we find that on June 30, 1966 there were 296,900 men available and qualified in the 1-A pool. By adding Selective Service's conservative estimates that 20,000 new 19-year-olds become draftable each month, we discover that on June 30 we were assured of 536,900 men available and qualified to meet the coming year's demands.

The pool held enough men to see us through another *entire* year of Vietnam-size draft quotas without calling up deferred men. Assuming draft calls had reached and remained at highs of 40,000 and 50,000—which they did not—it would have been at least January, 1967, before the 1-A pool became tight enough to warrant a second look at deferred men. In other words, Selective Service panicked at least one year too soon.

Finally, at the House hearings in June when the veracity of his shortage prediction was questioned, General Hershey admitted disarmingly: "So I was wrong in December." When reminded by Congressman William H. Bates of Massachusetts that the general had also predicted a shortage in March in a memo to Dirksen, General Hershey, with frustrating aplomb, passed off the matter as inconsequential. "I would be very happy to admit that I was still mistaken in March." Perhaps it is the arrogant unwillingness even to attempt explanation that makes General Hershey's admissions of error so disconcerting. One has the feeling his mistakes will continue interminably; that he will cheerfully admit them interminably; that we will suffer from them interminably; and, most nagging thought of all, that the General does not really consider them mistakes. It is difficult indeed to attack a man who refuses to defend himself, who humbly admits he fell victim to that human failing common to us all: He simply erred. But it is no tribute to our divinity, more probably proof of our guillibility, to readily forgive what the old General so candidly calls a "mistake"—a grievous mistake and irresponsibility which still keeps millions of young men and their families in a state of draft anxiety.

For there is still a widespread misconception that we are gripped by a manpower shortage, that we need to draft deferred men and are in fact drafting them in significant numbers. This is untrue. Our 1-A manpower pool is overflowing with men and is sufficient to meet draft needs for many months, if not years, under present demands. Early in 1967, draft calls dropped because requirements for Vietnam leveled off. Once troop build-up is complete, the draft picture changes. There is no longer the problem of supplying great numbers of "extra" men to bring the armed forces up to desired strength. The problem now (in spring 1967), unless there is further escalation, is merely to replace soldiers who are discharged. Unless the administration decides to raise the armed forces level above the 3.3 million of January, 1967, the following two years will not necessitate unusually high draft calls. The Labor Department estimates that if we hold forces at 3.3 million, we will need during 1967 only 600,000 new men (both enlistees and draftees), which is roughly the same number required in a normal, pre-Vietnam, year. The 1967 replacement needs will not be high, for we will be replacing men drafted in 1965, of which there were 233,000. Monthly draft calls should run less than 20,000, which is no drain whatever on the 1-A pool. In fact, even according to General Hershey's conservative estimates, at least 20,000 new nineteen-year-olds enter the 1-A pool every month. Nor should 1968 bring any semblance of a manpower crisis, although needs will be slightly higher. To maintain current strengths, 700,000 new soldiers will be needed in 1968, according to the Labor Department. This again should put no undue strain on the 1-A pool, considering that we supplied one million men in 1966—and the only manpower shortage we encountered was in the statistical imaginings of Selective Service.

Undeniably, Selective Service pushed the panic button needlessly. There was no manpower shortage that warranted inducting college students and other deferred men; the 1-A pool was not dwindling away; the Selective Service report, twice sent to Congress, was wrong.

Someone unfamiliar with Selective Service's operation perhaps might find nothing more significant in this than the slip of a statistician's pencil. And it is entirely possible that an honest statistical error may have truly alarmed Selective Service about unpredictable draft calls and a shortage that never developed. If so, this in itself warrants investigation into the competency of Selective Service's statisticians, who have our peace of mind at their mercy. We must remember that throughout 1966, neither the Labor Department nor the Pentagon manpower experts could find any immediate cause for alarm in the 1-A pool.

In eventual benefit to the draft, it matters little whether General Hershey leans against the panic button or pushes it intentionally. The rewards to the Selective Service System are approximately the same. For the System, unlike the American people, does not suffer when a "crisis mood" prevails. It benefits enormously. It has been said that "panic makes the draft go round," and, essentially, this is not an exaggeration.

An important but little appreciated fact is that the draft's power to stir up fear is inextricably tied up with the reason for its existence. Anyone who studies the draft soon discovers that it is not nearly so simple a mechanism as most Americans assume. The draft would be more comprehensible if it really were, as described by one writer, "a very simple mechanical computer [in which] the requirements go in at one end, and out come the bodies from the other." But the draft does not operate with such cold unemotionalism.

To the military, the draft's value is not measured, nor its existence justified, by how many men it brings in through regular draft channels; the draft's undisputed value lies in how many men it *frightens* into enlisting. The military counts on the fact, and rightly so, that a boy feeling the hot breath of the draft will often hasten to enlist in one of the services. Although the young man must serve three years as an enlistee, rather than the two years of a draftee, he believes the added benefits (choice of service, schooling and so forth) compensate for the extra year of service.

It is universally agreed that the primary purpose for the draft's existence is to generate enough fear to keep enlistments up. The more fear Selective Service can generate, the more valuable it is, General Hershey told me. "We're the recruiter's best friends," he said. "Enlistments depend on the fever throughout the country. The higher calls we announce, the higher the enlistments. If we announce calls of 5,000, enlistments go way down. If we say we'll take 80,000 men, enlistments go way up." Testifying before the House Armed Services hearings in June, 1966, Thomas D. Morris, Assistant Secretary of Defense, contended that we could not meet "foreseeable manpower requirements" without the draft because "it has long been apparent that the pressure of the draft has a decided influence on the decisions of many . . . who volunteer."

Congress and the Nation, a compendium of legislative history, noted that Congress extended the authority to draft in 1959 because: "As in 1955, supporters of the draft argued that its primary value lay in encouraging a sufficient number of volunteers to meet service manpower requirements. Again in 1963," the history continues, "there was minimum opposition to President Kennedy's request for a four-year extension to draft, although the Army expected to induct no more than 90,000 per year to maintain the authorized strength of 975,000. The major argument, as in the past, was that without it, the services held, voluntary enlistments would decline sharply."

Even those who most oppose the draft admit its scare techniques are effective. Arlo Tatum, executive secretary of the Central Committee for Conscientious Objectors, who was imprisoned during World War II and the Korean conflict for refusal to cooperate with the draft, deplores the use of the draft to panic young men into enlisting, but agrees: "It works."

It is not possible to ascertain precisely how much the draft's threat-power contributes to enlistments. A Selective Service official says: "For every one we draft, we chase in two others." Enlistments normally are twice as high as inductions; for example, 340,000 men were inducted in fiscal 1966, and about 600,-000 enlisted. But maintaining that the draft is responsible for every single enlistee is wishful thinking gone berserk.

A survey appraising the draft's effect on enlistments was cited by the Defense Department's Thomas Morris at the June House hearings. He reported the results of a questionnaire which asked servicemen: "Would you have entered the service if there had been no draft?" Thirty-eight per cent of the regular enlistees and 41 per cent of the officers said no, they would not have enlisted. A scholar who has intensively studied military manpower procurement, Walter Y. Oi, professor of economics at the University of Washington, maintains that without the draft, first-term enlistments would probably drop about 43 per cent for the Army and less for the other services.

In one profession, however, the draft's threat-tactics are nearly 100 per cent effective. Under a "doctor's draft" law passed in 1950, doctors, dentists and allied medical specialists can be called up individually because of profession, unlike any other occupational group in the country. Theoretically, doctors are not "drafted;" they are "persuaded" by Selective Service to enlist. It's the "bribe" and "scare" method, says General Hershey. "We scare them and the armed forces bribe them." According to a Selective Service spokesman, this is how the enlistment is accomplished. "The state headquarters issues a call for doctors, youngest first. The service to which the man is allocated sends him a letter and an application to notify him that if he volunteers he gets a captain's commission and $100 extra a month. His draft board tells him if he volunteers they will postpone his induction. We usually give him 20 days to act. If the doctors don't comply within 20 days—well, they have that induction order staring them in the face. This usually persuades them to join up." Understandably, this recruiting method has been eminently successful for, of course, if the medical man doesn't graciously accept his commission, he is drafted as a private. "We've only drafted three doctors in fifteen years," boasts Selective Service. The American Medical Association notes wryly that about 6,500 civilian doctors every two years have "enlisted."

Indecision, anxiety, uncertainty. These are the mental states General Hershey seeks to foster. Although most of us regard them as undesirable, they serve the draft's purpose. Selective Service hopes a boy will become so agitated that he will enlist rather than endure the uncertainty.

At the Chicago draft conference in December, 1966, Colonel Dee Ingold of Selective Service somewhat shocked participants by confessing that the draft consciously works to keep young men in a state of anxiety. "We do provide for uncertainty for a specific purpose," he said. "We produce this uncertainty to increase enlistments."

Selective Service's policy of fear-inspired guidance creates hardships for many boys and some ugly consequences for society. Young men, mainly because we draft the older men first, are caught in years of uncertainty, during which they cannot plan their futures. Although the average age of draftees today has dropped to twenty, before the Vietnam build-up it was much higher. In 1963, for example, the average age of men inducted was nearly twenty-four. This means that under normal circumstances, it is common for men to spend six years in draft uncertainty: many endure eight or more years with the draft a constant irritant in their lives.

Many draft-age men, especially those not enrolled in college, cannot find jobs or, at least, desirable ones. A Department of Defense survey showed that 39 per cent of the enlisted men who entered the services at ages twenty-two through twenty-five had been turned down for jobs because of their draft eligibility. Companies and employment agencies admit that boys who may be snatched away by the draft are unwanted. Said one agency in Detroit: "Many employers express the stipulation that employees be 4-F or have completed military training. It's rather prevalent as a stipulation."

Congressman Roman C. Pucinski summed up the predicament in a speech before the House in 1959. "I just completed a very intensive survey in Chicago on teenage gangs and juvenile delinquency, and I find that the draft has a very important effect on the present development of our young people. . . . Hundreds of thousands are forced to live in a shadow of constant doubt as to their future when actually only a few thousands are ultimately drafted. Many young men who graduate from high school and who do not, or cannot because of economic reasons, go to college find it impossible to get decent employment because the first thing they are asked by a potential employer is what is his draft status . . . I could not begin to tell you the hardships that this situation is causing."

The strain on college students is also considerable. A study on student stress by the National Student Association in 1965 revealed that nearly all male students suffer anxiety about the draft. They do not so much fear death or military regimentation; they resent that nagging feeling of never knowing "what's going to happen to us."

The military likes to have college students enlist for three years. General Hershey, too, likes to see college boys join up. Their enlistments enhance the draft's value to the military by bringing better-educated men into the services, deflecting criticism from student deferments as class privilege, and satisfying General Hershey's personal wish that students not escape service. Occasionally, Hershey also likes to have what he calls a "clean-up" of poorer students and those he thinks may be trying to escape the draft by prolonging their education.

Therefore, it should be no surprise that much of the phony manpower scare in early 1966 was aimed at college campuses. Through threat-techniques and the juggling of classifications, Selective Service made it look as if thousands of college students were in imminent danger of being drafted. It is true that some draft boards may have been as fooled by the mythical manpower shortage as the general public and may have actually drafted some full-time satisfactory students. But, for the most part, General Hershey did not really want to draft those students who would finish in four years; he much prefers frightening students, especially academic laggards, into enlisting.

As early as February 17, 1966, when the manpower scare was but a month and a half underway, Hershey told the Education Subcommittee of the House Education and Labor Committee that if draft calls stayed at 30,000 (which they generally did) there were no plans to draft full-time students. Nevertheless, many students were reclassified 1-A, causing a stir on many campuses. Some 1-A students were forced to resort to the one-time use of their 1-S classification. The college 1-S is an emergency classification which Congress decrees a board must issue to a student who is already attending classes to allow him to finish out the term, so he will not lose his tuition. At the end of the term, the board may reclassify the boy 1-A, making him uncomfortably vulnerable to the draft; for he can claim the 1-S only *once* during his college career. Whether or not the board will really draft him is another question, but if the anxiety is intolerable, he may fulfill his destiny in the draft's scheme by signing up "to get it over with."

The mere announcement of the college draft test is a powerful spur to enlistments. As Arlo Tatum says: "Many times it is not necessary for Selective Service to follow through on these tests, because so many get scared and volunteer before they can be drafted. This is the usual purpose for the test in the first place, so unfortunately, the procedure really works." College students, indeed, did respond to Selective Service's efforts to scare up enlistees. Only 11 per cent of the enlistees during the first six months of 1965 were college graduates or college dropouts. In April, 1966, more than twice that figure—26 per cent of the enlistees—were college men.

Real need is not the stuff Selective Service policies are made of. And we will little understand the draft if we continue to presume that their actions are always dictated by real manpower shortages. It is senseless, for example, to re-examine 70,000 previously deferred men over twenty-six to alleviate a manpower deficit. As one of Hershey's staff said: "Out of those we would get maybe 30,000; that's hardly enough to fill one draft call."

Threatening men over twenty-six was another stratagem to raise the country's draft fever and to satisfy General Hershey's personal social goals. He wanted to force young men into certain deferable occupations by instilling draft-fear (a process he calls "channeling," which is discussed fully in another chapter) and to warn college boys that they could not escape service by passing their twenty-sixth year. "That's why we're threatening these men," General Hershey told me. (Note the General's term is "threaten" not "draft;" he actually did want to induct them, but the military objected.) "The military doesn't really want these men. Now if they have a choice, who do you suppose they would rather have in Vietnam—a younger man or the ones over twenty-six? They want the younger boys. All we said, anyway, was that these boys ought to have another physical examination; that's all we asked draft boards to do. This is a signal for the graduate school boy if he's using college as a haven. It acts as a threat and a threat only."

Bill Mauldin, Pulitzer Prize-winning political cartoonist for the *Chicago Sun-Times,* recently pictured General Hershey swinging a lariat that spelled out "draft" around his head. A man tapping the General on the shoulder was saying: "Hey, General —that's a lasso, not a whip." Mauldin was criticizing the 1-A reclassification of fifteen University of Michigan students who staged a sit-in at an Ann Arbor draft board office. But his point holds true for the complete operation of the draft. It is decidedly not a lasso; it is a very powerful whip that lashes millions of men to extract a bit of blood-service from a few. The whipped need not even be the ones wanted by the military. The college students and over-twenty-sixes are thrown into anxiety although there is little intention of drafting them, to instill sufficient fear in younger men to induce them to enlist.

How far Selective Service will go in generating national unease to satisfy its goals is not known. But it seems certain that the announcement of a critical manpower shortage, coincidental with threats to college men and other deferred groups, would contribute substantially to a feeling of national draft-jitters, which in turn would stimulate enlistments and have other side-effects, desirable in the eyes of Selective Service, such as quieting criticism of the war. Is this the kind of deceit that we were served up by Selective Service when it announced a mythical manpower shortage in early 1966? In the absence of any other plausible explanation, save carelessness or gross incompetence, this is the only reasonable assumption to make.

4 ☆ The Draft Test Hoax

*"One's innate mental capacity should not be
a measure of his obligation to serve."*
—Senator Gaylord Nelson

It was in 1966—and still is—a purely academic question: If we are going to draft college students, which college students should we draft?

For twelve years (from 1951 to 1963) Selective Service provided the answer to this problem by using two criteria: 1) a 150-question multiple-choice test (similar to IQ and educational aptitude tests) called the Selective Service College Qualification Test and, 2) a boy's academic rank in his class. Only at the tail end of the Korean conflict did the question have life-and-death meaning. In 1963, the test and grade system was discontinued because, says General Hershey: "We were deferring everybody regardless of what their score was, so the test was a waste of time and money." Some years, fewer than 5,000 boys bothered to take the test.

When Hershey revived the test-rank procedure, effective March 23, 1966, he found a changed political climate. Hardly anyone, not even the administration, views Vietnam as "a splendid little war," as John Hay characterized the Spanish American War. Americans, made sharply sensitive to inequality by the civil rights movement, were indignant that a boy's brains should be the measure of his duty to serve and that he must compete with his classmates to determine who might be killed or forced to kill. Professors were especially outraged at becoming agents of the Selective Service System. Throughout the spring, controversy over what one newspaper called "a draft system of undemocratic lunacy" created general chaos.

"Let Selective Service do its own dirty work," said Leo Hanalian, dean of curricular guidance at City College in New York. Six professors at City College threatened to give A's to all students. At the University of Chicago, 150 professors, under the leadership of Richard Flacks, associate professor of sociology, signed a petition urging the noncooperation of colleges with Selective Service.

In June Detroit's Wayne State University took a courageous stand, initiated by its liberal president, William R. Keast. The university, he announced, as of the fall of 1966, would refuse to compile and release a boy's academic class standing to local boards.[1] Keast also attacked the test: "To put forth this test as valid is to perpetrate a fraud on the Selective Service System and the students. This silliness should be stopped, and it can be stopped by the educational community itself. If they would withdraw from being agents for the Selective Service System, reforming the system would be much simpler and could be done much more rapidly."

"Totally absurd," was how Dean Kermit Morrissey of Brandeis University appraised the test. Professor John Seeley, chairman of the sociology department at Brandeis, and six other sociologists denounced the tests as "a misuse of our role." Said Seeley, "I don't believe that the university can survive any further intrusion by the military. We have dirtied our hands enough with lucre. I don't want to see them dirtied by blood."

Although many students supported the testing, others objected vehemently. University of Chicago students picketed Science Research Associates, the educational firm in Chicago awarded the one-million dollar contract to draw up and administer the test. Students for a Democratic Society, which opposes the war and the draft, made up its own draft deferment test, called the National Vietnam Examination, which bore the names of a number of outstanding Americans, including Paul Goodman and Dr. Benjamin Spock. An SDS representative attempted to persuade Science Research Associates officials to substitute the Vietnam Test for the Selective Service Test. It made more sense in assessing a boy's fitness for Vietnam, he asserted.

Some publishers, counting on draft-fears to loosen a boy's pocketbook, rushed into print with dreary paperback books, full of tedious math and vocabulary problems, similar to those on the test. One book prompted a Harvard student to comment: "Anybody who would go through this thing just to take a 150-question test ought to be deferred for insanity."

The computers at Science Research Associates couldn't read students' handwriting on test application cards, and some students marked the wrong locality code number. Thus, machine and human errors produced weird mix-ups in assigning test locations. Thirty University of Michigan students were ordered to take their tests in Cambridge, Massachusetts. Ohio students were told to report to Oklahoma. Several Kentucky boys were told to pack up and go to Texas, and one was dispatched by the computer to Honolulu for the test.

Meanwhile, SRA carried on, taking elaborate security measures. They refused to disclose the name of the printer of the tests, locked up each question as it was developed, and made certain that no test-maker could sell his country's secrets. "Each psychologist making up the test did only a portion, and none saw the completed test in its entirety," reported SRA. Despite precautions, an Ohio Congressman charged that a carton of tests was left standing in a hallway of Western Reserve University where students could pilfer them. And in Texas, someone broke into a school and stole the tests. SRA promptly shipped off a new set of tests with different questions.

San Francisco State College refused to give the test on campus after a threat from the Vietnam Day Committee to disrupt the testing. Some University of Chicago students vowed to sabotage the whole affair by shouting out the correct answers.

In protest, 200 students at the University of Denver sat in the street and tossed eggs at policemen who tried to disperse them. At Chicago's Roosevelt University, twenty-five students were arrested during a sit-in at the administration building. University of Wisconsin protesters seized Bascom Hall, the administration building, during a night-time raid and kept control for eight hours. Students at Stanford University staged a forty-eight-hour protest and were subsequently placed on probation. For four days, some 700 demonstrators at the University of Chicago paralyzed university business by jamming the hallways and offices of the administration building.

On the test days, many universities lacked enough test papers and seats. One boy in New York was arrested and dragged out for tapping his key chain on the desk during the test. Other participants showed up with scribbled signs on their backs: "Score High or Die," and "Kill. It's good for the Economy." The crush was so great that Selective Service scheduled a fourth make-up test for June 24.

Students were marching. Professors were disturbed. Conscientious boys were agonizing over 150 questions which they believed would measure their brainpower and hence their chances of being drafted. And during these trying times, the maker of mayhem, General Hershey, was in Dallas, Texas, attending the annual meeting of the National Council of the Boy Scouts of America. On May 20, 1966—the day before 250,000 boys were to report for the second draft deferment test—Hershey made an extraordinary statement. He told an Associated Press reporter that few if any college students would be drafted. He affirmed that nonstudents and college drop-outs were sufficient to fulfill current military needs.

Such inconsistent remarks, even from the inconsistent General, are difficult to believe. Indeed, if college students did read them, they did not take them to heart. For boys turned out for the test in anticipated numbers—a total of 767,935 during the four test days.

General Hershey was in effect telling us that we were the victims of a monstrous government jest. Selective Service had no plans for drafting college students anyway, regardless of their test scores. This is the bitter, ironic point that was almost universally overlooked. The test, with its million-dollar tab, its marches, pickets, eggs and oratory, its tears and jeers, and chaos and general disruption of the educational process—was irrelevant, beside the point. There was no shortage of men in the I-A pool; hence there was no need to draft college students, nor, by the General's own admission, were there plans to do so.

Why then did the general let the testing continue? Once the test had been announced General Hershey apparently did not want to withdraw it—even as June neared and it became apparent that there was no deficit in the I-A manpower pool. General Hershey could have and should have cancelled the test, but it appears that he was determined from the start to have no interference. At the House Education and Labor Committee Hearings on February 17, 1966, Congressman Reid, skeptical of a manpower shortage, asked if the testing procedure could be reviewed before campuses were thrown into what might turn out to be needless turmoil. Hershey replied: "You leave me in a very awkward position, because I have to answer in the negative because we are already involved in letting contracts." Science Research Associates, however, reports that it was not awarded the contract until February 25, a week after the hearings.

The only justification General Hershey gave for going ahead with the test was that the results would be used in the future. At the hearings, he told Congressman Reid that the test scores would be employed to draft students to fill draft quotas in the fall. As we have seen, the fall of 1966 brought no manpower shortage, nor will the fall of 1967, short of a drastic escalation of war. Yet, Selective Service continues to administer the test. It was given in November, 1966, and was scheduled for April, 1967.

In October, prior to the test, I put the following questions to General Hershey:

> Question: General, do you plan to draft college students?
>
> Hershey: Well, now that depends on what you mean by student. Are you talking about the kid who goes to college in the fall and teachers with enthusiasm will throw him out at the end of the first semester? Is he a student? If he is, I'd say there's pretty good chance of drafting individuals who get pushed out of college at the end of their first quarter.
>
> Question: I wasn't thinking of dropouts. I meant full-time satisfactory students. Have any full-time satisfactory students been drafted?
>
> Hershey: There might be some—an exception here and there. But I'd say I haven't heard of students making satisfactory progress being taken out. Those aren't the kind of students being drafted.
>
> Question: Do you know of any student who has been drafted or reclassified 1-A as a result of his score on the deferment test?
>
> Hershey: Local boards have the authority on those things—
>
> Question: But have you personally heard of any such student being affected by the test?
>
> Hershey: No, I'd have to say I haven't.

In January, 1967, the deputy director of the Selective Service in Indiana told me that to his knowledge no boys in Indiana had been affected by the test. Major General Joe Nickell, director of the draft in Kansas, said they were generally deferring all full-time students, regardless of the test or class standing. In a survey of 15 other states made by the Associated Press in January,

1967, only one state—Mississippi—reported that either an acceptable class rank or a passing score on the draft test was mandatory for student deferments. According to the Associated Press, an Ohio draft official admitted that their boards sometimes disregard all four criteria (full-time status, academic progress, class rank and test score) "if we are having no trouble filling our quota in a particular month." Massachusetts draft officials said that their boards require no test standards or class rankings. "Students simply must be full-time, stay continuously in school and expect a degree in a reasonable amount of time." Arizona draft director, Norman L. Erb, reported that their boards follow national standards, "which means as long as the colleges continue to keep them in school, they're exempt."

It is true that some graduate students in "nonessential" fields of study (usually nonscientific or nonmedical) have been denied deferment and a few undergraduate boys have been drafted. Usually, however denials of the 2-S deferment have nothing to do with the test score or class standing. Typically, the undergraduates have been drafted at the end of a term for not making "satisfactory progress," which means they are taking more time than is normal to complete their education. Reports from Pennsylvania and New Jersey also indicate that so-called "troublemakers" who refused to take the test are being punished by having their 2-S taken away. It is also probable that a few isolated draft boards, acting independently of state and national policy, are actually applying the test-rank results and reclassifying or drafting boys on that basis. Nationally, however, the test scores and grades are almost universally ignored. The whole procedure then becomes meaningless and dishonest—a hoax on young men and professors who are led to believe that test scores and grades really do determine student deferment.

Educators believed in June, 1966 and still do that the test-rank plan is being seriously applied. This was evidenced by remarks of those attending the University of Chicago draft conference. When professor Richard Flacks was informed otherwise, he was disturbed. "That rather makes it a joke on us, doesn't it?" he said. And a cruel joke at that, for many professors agonized needlessly over the grades they issued.

Although General Hershey cannot be accused of lying, there is a sincerity gap between his insistence on giving the test and then not applying it. Some University of Chicago conferees, including John Naisbitt, an executive at Science Research Associates, expressed some suspicion that the test was a device to stir up anxiety among college students to increase enlistments. The charge was denied by the Selective Service representative to the conference, Colonel Dee Ingold. Another suspicion is that the test is used to foster the illusion of universality of service—making it seem that students along with other segments of the population are being drafted—and to lessen the criticism of student deferments as class privilege.

General Hershey should make it perfectly clear to the academic community that the test-grade criteria are *not being currently applied* to determine a boy's draft eligibility. It is inexcusable that he did not do this last spring. Such a clarification could have considerably ameliorated the turmoil surrounding the test. Since the test is still being given in the absence of any real manpower shortage, present or near-future, it would seem imperative that a Congressional inquiry determine just what General Hershey *is* using the test for.

The test-hoax is further compounded by the pretense that an acceptable score or class rank—within the criteria laid out by Selective Service—guarantees deferment. Purportedly, the deferment of college students is based on either a passing score of 70 (80 for graduate students) or satisfactory rank in class (upper half of freshman class, upper two-thirds of sophomore class, upper three-fourths of junior class). In truth, virtually all students making "satisfactory progress" are deferred. But even if the test-rank plan were being used as a basis for draft-board decisions, high scores and high marks would *not* assure deferment.

Most people are unaware that when the plan was instituted

Congress was so "unhappy about it," to quote General Hershey, that "they passed a law that said draft boards didn't have to pay any attention to the test or grades." Section 6(h) of the law, adopted in June, 1951, reads ". . . no local board, appeal board, or other agency of appeal of the Selective Service System shall be required to postpone or defer any person by reason of his activity in study, research or [medical] endeavors . . . solely on the basis of any test, examination, selection system, class standing . . . ."

Deferment of students is left by Congressional edict entirely up to the discretion of local boards. How broadly they may interpret the test score was revealed by General Hershey during the 1966 House Armed Services Committee hearings. After pointing out that 70 is a passing score, the General said: "But that doesn't prevent a local board from deferring a fellow at 65, if they feel here is a fellow that is unlucky, but who tried his best, and not deferring a fellow who got 90, but had a low class standing, because the board felt he could do better."

Later in the hearings, Congressman F. Bradford Morse of Massachusetts pursued this interpretive theory to its muddled conclusions: "Does this mean, as it implies, that a student who scores 72 on the qualification test and is in the lowest quarter of his class might be deferred by the same draft board because his test score and school work seem compatible? The General surely does not mean to suggest, either, that a student at a school with extremely high academic standards might not have a low class rank and a high score on the student qualification test.

"What is the sense," demanded Morse, "of establishing a class rank criterion and administering a student qualification test if there is no effort to assure that local draft boards will interpret the results the same way?"

We may justly complain that the test and class rank procedure is a fraud because it is not legitimately used as pretended. On the other hand, we can be thankful that the test and grades are *only* a fraud, that the semi-annual bombshells distributed to campuses are filled with confetti-threats and not the high explosives we are led to believe. For the test-grade system is discriminatory—both racially and academically—invalid, morally wrong and corruptive of the educational process. The educational community, which initiated the system, could and should see that it is abolished.

It is wrongly assumed that General Hershey had to storm his way into the institutions of higher learning with his draft-deferment plan. Rather, it was the educators who actually opened wide the doors of academia and ushered the General in. The test-rank criteria were suggested in 1949 by six Scientific Advisory Committees, as they were called, headed by M. H. Trytten, director of the Office of Scientific Personnel of the National Research Council. More than half, or fifteen out of twenty-six committee members, who signed the recommendation were educators—professors of science, humanities, medicine and business at leading universities. The plan was also endorsed by more than 550 educators at a meeting of the American Council on Education. The intent was to announce the new plan inconspicuously by a directive to local boards in March, 1949 (about nine months after the signing of the peacetime draft act). But President Truman believed such a grave departure from previous policies deserved the dignity of a White House announcement. He delayed his approval so that the test was not instituted until 1951, during the Korean War.

The Trytten committees, assembled to help Hershey implement the new draft act, were motivated to save the brightest students from the draft, especially the scientists. Despite the growing manpower surplus, it did not appear to committee members that *all* college students could or should be deferred. But it did seem imperative that *some* students be deferred. After reasoning that the brightest, most scholarly boys would presumably make the greatest contribution to society, the Trytten committees devised the test-rank plan to automatically select these promising young men for deferment. Congressman Curtis is harsh on the educators for their complicity: "They made a deal," he charges. "The college and universities said 'We won't resist if you will just leave us our bright boys.' As long as this pact exists we can't have an honest investigation of the draft. The educators won't allow it because they are afraid that the armed forces will take their best students. They are deliberately sacrificing the less able."

In 1966, the educational establishment again gave their blessing to the test. The American Council on Education on its own initiative urged Selective Service to reinstate it. When I asked Dr. Harrison Sasscer, program director of the Association of American Colleges, why colleges stood for the intrusion of the draft when they are supposedly so sensitive to invasions of academic freedom, he replied: "What's the alternative? In a situation like World War II [when every man is needed] it's simple, but in a situation like the Korean War, the alternatives are more unpleasant. They'll say scientists are useful, so we will exempt scientists and take the humanists, which is something we couldn't tolerate very long. We begged them to go back to the test as the least disagreeable solution. We had to knock them over the heads to get the test back, because we were afraid that the local boards will begin to do as they damn please."

Many educators, however, are unwilling to abide by the pact made in their names with Selective Service. They find it abominable. Morris Janowitz, professor of sociology, University of Chicago, calls it "incredible" that the American Council on Education endorsed the test and class rank without consulting its constituents more widely in view of "changed political circumstances and heightened sensitivity to issues of social justice." An executive at Science Research Associates said that "given the social climate of today, a re-examination of the test policy is not entirely a bad thing—long overdue in my personal opinion." SRA, in fact, decided to wash its hands of the whole affair. It was not an accident that after the June, 1966 tests, SRA "lost" the contract to Educational Testing Service in New Jersey. "It just so *happened* that our bid was too high," said an SRA spokesman.

To professors, the more horrifying aspect of the "Trytten plan" is drafting boys on the basis of grades. The university or college computes the boy's academic rank with all full-time male students in his class—for example, he might be 124 out of a freshman class of 420—and provides the information to local boards. The onus of selecting draftees then indirectly falls on the teacher, corrupting his role and his relationship with students. The difference between a C and D may determine whether a boy drops into the bottom half of his class, and thus theoretically is subject to the draft.

Surely, professors have a right to object to giving life-and-death grades. One young professor said: "Is this why I became a teacher?" Paul M. Harrison, associate professor of religious studies at Pennsylvania State University, pointed out that "it will require either superhuman wisdom or demonic indifference for a professor to decide whether a borderline student should pass or fail if, in failing, he is subject to the draft. [We should] unequivocally refuse to be used as the political instrument of the state."

Educators are aware that grades are variable from professor to professor, school to school (an A at Harvard is decidedly more significant than one at Kent State) and are highly unreliable in assessing a student's ability and learning progress. It is dangerous and absurd to tie national policy to grades, "perhaps the weakest and certainly the most easily abused feature of education," in the words of Norman Cousins, editor of the *Saturday Review*. Cousins, like many educators, fears that the renewed emphasis on high marks, created by Selective Service, is educationally destructive, discourages student experimentation and freezes schools in the lockstep of the grading system from which many are trying to escape. Young men corrupt their educational plans by choosing major fields and easy courses in which they are assured of making high grades. A boy who would like to take music appreciation may instead enroll in first-aid to make that high grade he believes essential to draft-avoidance. "Emphasis on high marks serves to create an atmosphere in which the infinite possibilities of learning are obscured and sometimes blocked," writes Cousins. "When top grades become the summit of education, the school falls to the bottom of its possibilities." [2]

The draft test also is academically unsound. It favors students in scientific fields. Undeniably, the Trytten committees had a scientific bias which is betrayed by the very word 'scientific' in the committees' name. Part of the reason for their existence was to save scientists for national defense. The atomic age brought a new reverence for scientists, a new sense of their worth to the military and a kind of remorse that some of our best scientific brains might have been blown out on the beaches of Normandy or Guadalcanal. The scientific community was determined that such a waste should not occur in future wars.

In fact, many scientists, including some on the Trytten committees', wanted automatic deferment for *all* students in scientific and engineering fields. They also wanted the power to draft science students removed from Selective Service and given to a separate manpower board. This attempt to diminish his domain galled General Hershey and he defeated the proposal. Still, today we see the bias of the committees reflected in their choice of a draft test which favors the scientifically minded. This is not to say that the test is intentionally made up to be discriminatory; but a committee that set out to defer promising artists or writers or teachers would choose selection criteria other than a general scholastic achievement test like the SSCQT; they might, say, use separate aptitude tests for different talents.

It was obvious from the beginning that an artist would not score as high as a scientist on the draft qualification test. Thus, in times of war, the test would leave future scientists safely ensconced in the halls of ivy while future artists, poets, musicians, historians, teachers—who enrich our lives, but whose talents do not lie in this particular kind of test taking—would be sent off to battle as sacrificial surrogates. If used in peace, the test is equally unfair, freeing the scientifically minded from service while forcing the brunt of military duty on boys who prefer non-scientific pursuits.

Even General Hershey admits that the "examination only has the appearance of being fair. It tends to get cocked over toward the mathematical because it's easier to grade, for one thing. This means the mathematicians or scientists have a better chance of making it than the liberal arts or 'Ags' [agriculture students] or educators." [3]

The May, 1966 Selective Service test showed this to be true. According to a 10 per cent sample, students in the physical sciences and mathematics made the highest scores, in the 88th percentile. Next were humanities students in the 86th percentile; social science, history and law students, 83rd percentile; biological sciences, medical and engineering students, 82nd percentile; general arts, business and commerce students, 79th percentile; agriculture and education students, 78th percentile. It is of further interest to note that although many students in seven major fields failed the test, not a single physical science, math or engineering student in the sample failed to achieve the passing score of 70.[4]

Before the draft test was given in May, 1966, Representative Adam Clayton Powell, of New York, with characteristic flamboyance, called the test reminiscent of Hitler and suggested that each test paper be engraved at the top with a swastika. His main concern, as usual, centered on racial inequality. He predicted that an "excessively disproportionate number of those failing would be black students." Said Powell: "The draft deferment test brings the circle of racial discrimination full cycle. First, we provide an inferior education for black students. Next we give them a series of tests which many will flunk because of an inferior education. Then we pack these academic failures off to Vietnam to be killed."

Some people regarded his prediction as Powell histrionics. But when the tabulations of those passing were made public, they did indeed show a discrimination against Negroes. Of the 767,935 boys who took the test in the spring of 1966, 624,436 of them made a passing score of 70 or better. Fully 81 per cent passed, which incidentally reveals how easy the test was. (An official at SRA said, "Of course, we didn't made the test very difficult. Selective Service *wants* almost everyone to pass so they will have reason to defer them.") SRA also admits that the test is culturally weighted to favor the white, middle-class and upper-class student, as are all tests of this type.

A 10 per cent sample of the 1966 test showed that in New England with its prestigious universities, only 7 per cent of the students failed. In the Middle Atlantic area, including New York, New Jersey and Pennsylvania, students did only slightly worse; 9 per cent failed. In the Midwest and Far West, from 12 to 16 per cent made below 70.

In the deep South, with its prevalence of Negro colleges, the scores were low. In Arkansas, Louisiana, Oklahoma and Texas, 32 per cent of the students failed the test. In Alabama, Kentucky, Mississippi and Tennesee, 47 per cent failed.[5] If this test were applied to choose our soldiers, we would draft Negroes from poorer southern colleges and leave our white boys at Yale and Harvard. As a professor pointed out, such an anti-Negro test might well be an unlawful violation of civil rights, as well as a violation of moral justice.

Even if all other conditions were perfect and the nation agreed that boys with the brightest futures should be deferred, the test-rank system used by Selective Service would still be deficient. It is based on a faulty premise. It assumes that young men who make the best grades in college and score highest on the draft test, which is an educational aptitude test similar to the college board exam, will become the most successful in their chosen fields. In his book *Student Deferment in Selective Service,* which explains the theory behind the test-rank policy, Trytten writes confidently that students in the top quarter of their classes will be "more competent and successful in individual specialities after graduation," than those ranking in the quarter below, and that those in the second quarter will enjoy more future success than those in the third quarter, and so on down the line, the boys at the bottom of the class being voted by Trytten "least likely to succeed," and thus less entitled to deferment because they will make the least contribution to society.

The very year, 1952, that Trytten's theories of "scholar finish first" was published, Dwight D. Eisenhower was elected to the highest office in the land, became commander in chief of the armed forces and head of the Selective Service System that Trytten sought to reform. Eisenhower in 1915 finished barely in the top third of his West Point graduating class. Under the Trytten plan, currently in effect, Thomas A. Edison and Albert Einstein, both considered dull by their teachers, and Ernest Hemingway, who failed freshman English, would have been thrown to the military as unfit college material.

Trytten—himself a scientist—and his committees formulated the draft deferment policies on no scientific evidence whatever. Nor have the advocates of the test-ranking procedure since been able to produce any. In February, 1966, Dr. Bowen C. Dees, associate director for planning of the National Science Foundation, testifying before the education subcommittee of the House Labor and Education Committee, cited the traditional reason that students who score high on the test and "do well in their studies should be deferred because this gives evidence they can make a real contribution." When pressed by Mrs. Edith Green, chairman of the subcommittee, Dr. Dees could cite not a whit of evidence to support his assumption. He conceded that the National Science Foundation did not possess any such evidence.

The reason is simple: There is none. In fact, current research shows that a straight A student does not necessarily make a greater contribution than a C student. (President Kennedy, for example, is said by college friends to have maintained a "gentleman's C" average.) In 1964, a team of University of Utah professors reported to the American Association of Medical Colleges that medical students with poor grades frequently become very successful doctors. Their study concluded that there is almost no relationship between the grades a student gets in medical school and his competence and success in medical practice.[6]

A 1964 study by Professor Eli Ginzberg and his associates at Columbia University of 342 fellowship winners showed startlingly that high scholarship was more likely to lead to comparative failure than success. Fifteen years after graduation, the students who had graduated with honors, had won medals or prizes, had been the Phi Beta Kappas, were more likely to be in the lower professional achievement levels than in the top levels. To further turn the Selective Service theories topsy-turvy, Ginzberg found that students with no undergraduate honors of any kind were more likely to be post-college successes than those singled out for scholastic distinction. Most destined for success were students with above average ability and outstanding personalities.[7]

The draft test has been proved no more valid in predicting tomorrow's successes than college grades have. The test, like most of its type, penalizes the perceptive or knowledgeable student. One sample question from the draft test prepared by SRA was the second verse of a poem from *A Shropshire Lad* by A. E. Housman. It read in part:

> Now, of my threescore years
> and ten,
> Twenty will not come again,
> And take from seventy springs
> a score,
> It only leaves me fifty more.

The student was then asked: How old was the poet when he wrote this poem?

> A—20   D—70
> B—40   E—One cannot tell
> C—50

The testmakers unimaginatively assumed that the poem had to be autobiographical, and noted the correct answer as A. In truth, the poem was published in 1896 when Housman was about thirty-seven. Obviously, the question was poorly phrased, and should have read "How old does the poet say he is?" As a New York professor pointed out in a letter to General Hershey, "The question was conceived as an exercise in translating English into mathematics." A young man who knew that reading poetry entailed more than counting would have correctly given E (one cannot tell) as the answer, but his intelligence would have cost him a few points.

A nationally known psychology professor, Dr. Karl U. Smith, University of Wisconsin, calls the draft test fraudulent, misleading and totally unscientific. "It has no proven validity in predicting scholastic or academic talent . . . it has been made up through guesswork, is being administered as guesswork and will be scored as guesswork in determining the college students who will live and die in Vietnam," charges Professor Smith. He thinks that all students and parents of students should be warned that any boy "in volunteering to take the test in order to avoid the draft, is being subjected to a scientific hoax."

5 ☆ Privileged *Not* to Serve

In 1951, when provisions for student deferments were being worked out, one Congressman seriously proposed that every deferred student should wear a distinguishing insignia as a badge of honor. Today, if that proposal had passed, we would have on our campuses a monumental, readily recognizable fraternity of 2-S boys, some 1.7 million strong. Student deferments are hardly the privilege of the chosen few. Virtually all full-time satisfactory students, regardless of their field of study, are deferred from military service in the name of the "national interest."

According to Section 6(h) of the Universal Military Training and Service Act, the President is authorized to defer anyone "whose activity in study, research, or (medicine) or other endeavors is found to be necessary to the maintenance of the national health, safety, or interest." The inherent problem in implementing this law is immediately apparent. What is the meaning of "necessary to the national health, safety or interest?" There is no fixed definition of this phrase. It is subject to wide and personal interpretation, and under existing regulations, the phrase means whatever General Hershey and the local boards deem it to mean at any specific time.

In all-out war, the traditional definition of "necessary" is clear. Students, then, are deferred from military service only if the subject they are studying is so vital to the war effort that they are *needed* more as students than as soldiers (chemists, physicists, aeronautical engineers, etc.). But when the nation is not threatened by extinction, who among us is philosopher-king enough to decide which individuals are most "necessary" to the national good? General Hershey, whom we have unwittingly authorized to make such choices, arbitrarily has decided that students, rather than non-students, are more "necessary" to society. He defers as "necessary" those students studying anything —from physical education to classical Greek. When asked at the House Armed Services Committee hearings why college students were deferred, Hershey replied: "Well, the theory, for whatever it may be worth, is that a college graduate is a more—has more possibilities of being a good citizen than one who is not a college graduate. That could very well be contradicted. But the whole philosophy of student deferment is based upon the theory that a student who graduates is of more use than one who does not graduate." [1]

As the general suggests, this theory can be seriously questioned. None of these modern figures received college degrees: George Romney, Ernest Hemingway, Charles Lindbergh, John Glenn, William Faulkner, Jackson Pollock, Henry Ford, Robert Frost, David Sarnoff.

Furthermore, can't we say that carpenters, plumbers and auto mechanics are also "necessary" to our safety? Aren't hospital orderlies necessary to our health? Isn't it possible that civil rights workers may be contributing more to the future interest of America than accounting students? It seems doubtful that the nation as a whole would endorse General Hershey's philosophy that a college diploma makes a boy's life worth more.

Void of a clear definition of "necessity" and "national good," student deferments become meaningless. The situation is an absurdity akin to asking our courts to interpret the "national good" without any code of laws whatever. The national good, obviously, is subject to a thousand interpretations. There are some, including this writer, who believe that Selective Service itself undermines the national health, safety and interest. In writing this book, I believe I am contributing to the nation's welfare, but it is doubtful that General Hershey will agree.

Even if we do agree that higher education is desirable, can we seriously maintain that it is essential to the extent of one and a half million male students? That it is vital to national survival that they remain on campus? That the nation would face ruin if 10 per cent, 25 per cent, 50 per cent were inducted into the armed forces for two years?

Participants at the December, 1966 University of Chicago conference gave serious thought to student deferments, and were willing to consider arguments for both sustaining and abolishing the 2-S. As the discussion proceeded, it became apparent that although the group sought an explanation for the 2-S classification, those attending, including Selective Service representative Colonel Ingold, could not present what appeared to be solid justification for deferment of all students. Geoffrey C. Hazard, Jr., professor of law at the University of Chicago, said he would like to "boldly suggest that the only justification for medical students' deferments is to legitimatize drafting them as doctors." Dr. Harold Wool, director of procurement policy, office of the Assistant Secretary of Defense for Manpower, admitted that the Pentagon saw no virtue in deferring all college students, but supported some student deferments to provide the military with specialists, such as doctors and engineers, who could later be drafted.

But even without deferments, only a small fraction of students would be drafted; it hardly seems likely that the supply of potential doctors, scientists or other highly skilled personnel would be critically diminished. At least, the conferees did not think so. An

overwhelming number signed a petition to abolish student deferments.

The Selective Service rationale for widespread student deferments is so unsupportable that General Hershey is caught in
constant contradiction trying to defend the policy. When I questioned him, he justified the 2-S by saying: "Where do you think
this moon business would be without the people who have been
trained under deferments for the last fifteen years? Some 550,-
000 have become engineers in that time." When I noted that the
argument was not valid because all students, not only those in
critical areas, had been deferred, the general agreed: "Yes, but
that's because we have a production of 1.8 million kids a year
and 150,000 a month. When calls were 5,000 where do you
think the other 145,000 will go? You see, you had to do something, and you'd better try to encourage them to go to school
rather than encourage them not to."

The key phrase in the general's statement is "you had to do
something."

In those words, rather than in the law or any grand national
purpose, lies the real reason behind student deferments: they are
necessary to hold back the oversupply of young men who would
otherwise glut the 1-A pool. The general had too many men on
his hands—so he sent them to college. Bluntly, student deferments are one of the many hypocrisies foisted on us by men
desperate to shore up the Selective Service System. It is small
wonder that the University of Chicago conferees, unaware of
this fact, were completely baffled in their search for a logical
reason behind the 2-S.

Colonel Ingold of Selective Service, noting the consensus to
abolish student deferments, expressed amazement at the participants' naïveté and predicted the outcome: "Even if you deny
boys the 2-S, the armed forces can't take them; they will be deferred anyway. They will be deferred as 1-A."

Thus, Selective Service is caught in the hypocritical position
of pretending that 1.7 million college boys are so necessary to

the nation's welfare that they can't be spared for the military, while at the same time admitting that the military doesn't want them. These million and a half boys are *not necessary* to the national welfare; they are *not necessary* to the military establishment. They are necessary only to the preservation of Selective Service. College boys are not deferred for the national good, but simply at the whim of Selective Service officials who want to keep the draft operating. This injustice is an affront to the human sensibilities of all Americans.

It is not surprising that student deferments are at the center of the current storm over the draft. Special draft treatment, such as that accorded students, has always been abhorrent. The arrogant exemption of the rich in the Civil War (even Abraham Lincoln kept his son at Harvard) incited the working class to bloody riots. In World War I, the blanket exemption of shipyard workers caused a near-scandal for Selective Service. Congressmen and draft officials are fully aware of American antagonism toward special privilege and group exemption of any sort. Yet, against all warnings of history, in their efforts to save Selective Service, they have created an elite corps of college boys, most of whom will never see military duty.

Student deferments are no longer just postponements of service, as once intended; they are now exemptions. It is true that the armed forces draws nearly all its doctors and about ninety per cent of its officers from among the graduates of civilian colleges, and that many young college boys, notably 2nd Lieutenant platoon leaders, are killed in Vietnam. Nevertheless, the statistics decidedly prove that men with college degrees are a privileged group—far less likely to be drafted than their compatriots.

According to a Selective Service survey of 1964 registrants, of the men twenty-six years old, fifty per cent who attended high school but did not graduate served; sixty per cent of all high school graduates and those with some college education served. In comparison, only forty per cent of the college graduates served.[2] These figures, although they do indicate that fewer college graduates serve, do not give a true picture of the extent to which they escape service. The Selective Service percentages are misleading because they lump together the military experience of men who served in the reserves, including the National Guard, with that of men who saw active duty. Although service is service, equating reserve duty with two or three years of active duty (particulary when we are fighting a shooting war) does not seem cricket. When the active duty service of college boys is analyzed, they do not fare so well. Prof. Walter Oi studied the same age group surveyed by Selective Service—men who were twenty-six in 1964. Oi separated the active duty veterans from the reservists. He determined that while 58 per cent of the high school graduates had seen active duty, only 36 per cent of the college dropouts and a mere 26 per cent of the college graduates had been on active duty.[3]

The figures in both Oi's and the Selective Service's studies included volunteers as well as draftees. If we consider draftees alone, the small percentage of college graduates who are drafted is a near scandal. The most conclusive proof of the draft's flagrant discriminatory policies is found in a 5 per cent sample survey of the Army's draftees on active duty as of February 28, 1966. The study showed that 24 per cent of the men drafted into the Army were high school dropouts; 62 per cent were high school graduates, and 12 per cent were college dropouts. *Only 2 per cent of all the men drafted had college degrees.*[4] These figures, which reflect the true and outrageous class bias of the draft, are almost never mentioned by draft officials.

Men are being killed in Vietnam, and it is morally unjustifiable for a society to shift the brunt of war duty to boys who cannot or do not wish to go to college. Many Americans, particularly the white middle-class officials who make draft policy, may regard education as the sacred hope of the nation and see nothing unjust in "rewarding those who better themselves," to quote General Hershey. Many boys want to go to college; on the other hand, many do not, and are actually better off in jobs than on the campuses where the draft has chased them because of General Hershey's questionable philosophy that a college degree makes them more valuable. It does seem in a democracy that we must preserve a boy's freedom of choice, by honoring his right *not* to go to college as well as his right to go. Since we have no laws commanding a boy to achieve a higher education, it is surely an outrage that the government can punish him, threaten his very existence by saying: "All right, if you will not or cannot go to college, then you will fight our wars." As Paul Goodman demanded of a group of college freshmen, "Why should Negro and Puerto Rican boys be fighting in the rice paddies of Vietnam while you're sitting safely here?"

The student exempted or deferred, possibly until termination of the Vietnam war, often has no inherent superior qualities save the fortuitous accident of having been born to a father of some means. Student deferments rightly carry the stigma of socio-economic privilege. Some defenders of present policy argue that many poor boys go to college on scholarships and by working part-time. This is true, although it is less true under a recent Selective Service edict that forbids deferments for boys carrying a part-time course load. Even boys trying to work their way through college must take the *full* number of hours or expose themselves to the draft.

Moreover, poor boys in college are more the exception than the rule. Higher education is still primarily a privilege of the middle and upper classes. In California, for example, only 5 per cent of the college students come from families with annual incomes of less than $4,000.

It is also undeniable that a determined father with enough cash can buy deferment by finding a college of some kind in which to install his son. During the House hearings in June, one Congressman cited the example of Parsons College in Fairfield, Iowa, which has been called "Flunk-Out U" and a college for "rich, dumb kids," because it allegedly accepts draftable wealthy boys who have failed in other colleges. Parsons, a

twelve-year-old private college, has a student body of nearly
five thousand (80 per cent men), runs at 87 per cent capacity during the summer (keeping draft-eligible boys in college), charges $1,650 tuition a year, and reportedly does not
consider rock-bottom grades sufficient reason for expulsion. A
twenty-year-old boy who said he enrolled at Parsons because
"the Army was after me," reported that one group of 197 dor-
mitory men had an aggregate average on finals of only 0.80.
"Twenty-one guys got 0.00," he said. "There's no stigma if you
screw up and have money too. In most schools they knock you
for that." But at Parsons, he explained: "Nobody sweats. Nobody gets axed." Asked why draft boards don't look into the
state of affairs, Parsons' president, Dr. Millard G. Roberts said:
"The only criterion [for deferment] really is whether he's making progress. If he nudges up his grade point one-tenth of a per
cent, that's progress, isn't it?" [5]

The Harvard Crimson of May 7, 1966, called the 2-S deferment provision, "one of the clearest examples of class-privilege
legislation in American history." In his baccalaureate address in
June, Harvard's president Nathan M. Pusey gently chided the
Crimson for not viewing the 2-S in historical perspective. Said
Pusey, "surely the 2-S was not designed as 'class privileged legislation!' " He is quite right, but in 1940, when student deferments were debated in the House, some Congressmen, with
remarkable prescience, feared that the provision would become
a means of evading service and would be condemned as class
legislation. Congressman Dewey Short of Missouri opposed student deferments, as a "storm cellar," where young men could
hide from the draft. "Why," he asked, " should the poor man
and the poor man's son who have been denied the privileges
of education and have not enough financial support to enroll in
a college or university be inducted and drafted, whereas another
young man can succeed in scraping enough money together to
enroll in order that he may be exempted or his service may be
deferred?" So many Congressmen shared Short's view that his

amendment, which would have killed student deferments, was voted down by a squeaky margin of only three votes—124 to 127.[6]

Some Congressmen at the time even condemned the deferments as an outrageous act of paternal selfishness by legislators to protect their own sons. Congressman Karl E. Mundt of South Dakota, said, "It is hard for me to understand why a mechanic learning a trade, a farm boy practicing his pursuit or a young professional man just getting a foothold in life should be treated any differently from the freshmen at Yale and Harvard whose fathers have been so eloquent and so vigorous in drafting and supporting this bill. Since these exemptions thus include practically all sons of Congressmen and Senators, it seems to me that providing for them is an especially demoralizing practice in a Republic which has never condoned before anything smacking of class legislation." He reminded his colleagues that "We cannot expect to increase respect for Government when the people's representatives in Congress insist in writing into law exemptions from a conscription law which will defer the draft as it affected their own sons, but direct its application with correspondingly increased severity to the sons of their less well-situated constituents."[7]

That legislators' sons are still protected by the "class privilege legislation" was exposed in the November, 1966, issue of *Ramparts* magazine. It conducted a "quiet survey in August" and reported that "A total of one hundred and forty-six senators and congressmen have one or more sons between the ages of eighteen and twenty-six—there are a total of one hundred and ninety-one such sons in all. *Ramparts* was able to track down the whereabouts of all but thirteen of them. Of the one hundred and seventy-eight thus accounted for, only sixteen were serving in the Armed Services, and only one was in Vietnam.

"The one young man serving in Vietnam was Clarence Long, Jr., son of Maryland Congressman Clarence Long. Long, twenty-two years old, was a paratrooper with the Special Forces, who obviously wanted to be where he was. The other fifteen were mainly commissioned officers (graduates of the service academies and products of ROTC) or had enlisted in the Navy or the Air Force. Apparently, none had been drafted."

To some, especially those who passionately believe in the un-questioned good of education, it may be unthinkable that Con-gressmen might indulge in such hypocrisy or that the population would seriously accuse them of such. But hypocrisy need not be conscious to be present; the mind is capable of many rationaliza-tions when one's son is in danger or when one's class values are challenged. Consciously or not, aren't Congressmen in effect saying to men whose draftable sons are not in college, "My boy's life is more valuable than your boy's"? We should be aware that many Americans do view it that way and strongly resent the immunity of Congressmen's sons from the draft. On a Chicago question-and-answer radio show in December, 1966, Roman C. Pucinski, Illinois Congressman, was challenged by an irate caller who demanded: "Why do you send our boys to Vietnam and keep your own at home?" When Pucinski weakly explained that many Congressional colleagues had asked him to say hello to their soldier-sons when he made a recent trip to Vietnam, the informed caller pressed: "Who?" When Pucinski referred to Congressman Long's son, the caller demanded "Who else? Who else? Tell me the names of the others!" Pucinski, of course, could not name any.

Student deferments clearly constitute class privilege. How-ever, to condemn the 2-S solely on this basis misses part of the point. The offensiveness is not entirely that deferred boys come from the upper socio-economic strata, although indeed it is compounded by this factor. It is likely that Americans, as sug-gested by their antagonism toward exempted ship-builders in World War I, would be incensed by the blanket deferment of any group, regardless of its members' financial-social creden-tials. Wouldn't we also find it objectionable to defer the sons of all miners, farmers or steel workers? Concentration on the class privilege aspect of student deferments obscures the democratic principle that we consider *all* group deferments morally wrong —so wrong that they are forbidden by the Selective Service Act.

It is rarely called to public attention that the blanket deferment of students is illegal. Section 6(h) of the draft law reads: "No person within any such category [study and occupation] shall be deferred except upon the basis of his individual status." In other words, no group deferments are allowed. During World War II, Selective Service guarded scrupulously against violating this law. Communiqués to local boards regarding students consistently warned that "Under no circumstances was the board to deviate from the clear statutory prohibition against group deferment."

Today, one would not know that the law existed. Selective Service brazenly defers 1.7 million boys solely because they are students; this is group deferment, contrary to the law. The illegality of blanket student deferments also raises another suspicion about General Hershey's illogical insistence on the college draft test and ranking plan. Do the tests and grades help mask the illegality of student deferments by fostering the illusion that each student is considered on an individual basis—his test score and grades?

When I asked General Hershey if the test-rank were used to cover up the illegality of blanket student deferments, he gave a negative answer by way of parable, as he often does. Hershey said: "For instance, a man is standing at a door like one of those swinging doors. There might be people he didn't let through the door. Now all the people who were inside came through the door, but that doesn't mean that everybody who was outdoors came through the door. And even if everybody did, they did so individually; they didn't go through collectively. What I'm trying to say is, every person who gets deferred to go to school gets deferred individually by an individual board."

And soldiers do not constitute the armed forces because they were inducted individually, and Negroes are not discriminated against as a group as long as society rejects them one by one, and physicians at a conference of the American Medical Association are not a group of doctors because they each showed their badge at the door, and Americans do not a nationality make, because our birth certificates were stamped individually by clerks at the board of health—as routinely as clerks in local draft boards mark 2-S on student files.

Clearly, by General Hershey's definition there can be no groups at all, for groups are made up of individuals, individually admitted, and that they came in one by one has no bearing at all on their ultimate composition. Students need only that one common ticket of admission to General Hershey's group deferment plan: a certificate of college registration. That they show it to different ticket-takers is of little significance. Inside, they are students, one and all.

Because so many middle and upper class students are escaping service, it does not follow that the burden then falls more heavily on the poor—that the poor are deliberately sent off as "cannon fodder" for the war in Vietnam. This is a myth that nevertheless has received wide publicity. Actually, the disadvantaged, especially nonwhites, are more privileged *not* to serve than the so-called privileged. According to a 1964 Pentagon study, of the men aged twenty-seven to thirty-four who had less than an eighth-grade education, only 30 per cent had ever been in the armed forces. Those from lower economic groups are often so educationally impoverished that they cannot pass the armed forces qualifying test (AFQT).

Contrary to popular belief, the Negro is notably *excluded* from the draft. According to a figure reluctantly released by the Department of Defense in October, 1966, an astounding 67.5 per cent of all Negroes fail the armed forces qualifying test and thus cannot enlist or be inducted. This figure compares with

18.8 per cent of white Americans who fail the test. The failure rate was demonstrably higher in the South; South Carolina has the highest Negro failure rate: 85.6 per cent.[8]

The percentage of Negroes drafted fluctuates from year to year, reports the Pentagon. The total Negro population is about eleven per cent. In 1965, the percentage of nonwhites among those drafted was sixteen per cent. In fiscal 1966, the percentage was eleven per cent, commensurate with the population. Reportedly, in the last ten years, the number of Negro draftees averaged about eleven to twelve per cent, indicating that we are not drafting a disproportionate number of Negroes.

The confusion that led to charges of racial discrimination in the draft came from the casualty figures in Vietnam. During 1965, 23.5 per cent of all Army enlisted men killed in Vietnam were Negroes. This reflects not a bias in the draft but the sickness of a society that offers its black citizens so little that they are forced to prove their manhood and fatten their paychecks by risking their lives in volunteer combat units. The Negro often finds more security, acceptance and educational opportunity inside the service than out. His re-enlistment rate in the Army after the first tour of duty is 49 per cent; as compared to 19 per cent for whites. He also is frequently a "double volunteer," choosing hazardous duty, such as the paratroops or Special Forces that warrants extra pay, and can cost his life.

If there is any socio-economic group of boys who deserve our sympathy, it is the ones not deprived enough to fail the army's mental test and not fortunate enough to be enrolled in college —the boys who get out of high school and go into a nonessential job. These are the boys most unfairly treated—the ones shouldering the guns for us—the ones squeezed into service by the draft's despicable policies of setting standards so artificially high that men on the lower socio-economic scale are exempted, and then deferring all those students on the upper end. The men in the middle suffer. In effect, Selective Service allows and encour-

ages the boys with the brains, money and educational aspira-
tions to buy their way out and send a substitute from the working class to Vietnam, in a style reminiscent of the Civil War.

6 ☆ Local Boards: An Anachronism

*"I know very well that most local boards will
defer someone who's in premedic or medical
school before they will defer the liberal-arts
man. I know they'll defer a scientist before
somebody who is teaching music . . .
Biology is give and take. Sometimes they
think these biologists are going to be in a
position to kill everybody in the world, and
they'll go a long way to defer one. Sometimes
they don't know what biology is—if they
think it's botany, they won't go so far."*

—Lieutenant General Lewis B. Hershey,
U.S. News and World Report,
January 10, 1966

Time has left Selective Service untouched. A visit to the Selective Service headquarters at 1724 F. Street, Washington, D.C., is like returning to the age of Dickens. In the six-story gray building and its brick annex across the street you can find aging men bent over ill-lit desks, surrounded by old wooden filing cabinets. Painstakingly, by hand, they record figure after figure on large yellow ledger sheets that cover their desk tops and hang over onto the floor. These men are keeping track of our 33 million draft registrants with *pencil and paper*. General Hershey does not allow computers; he does not believe in them. (He does allow adding machines, I am told, although I did not see any. I did see Xerox machines.)

Selective Service is hopelessly out of date. Its existence, its philosophy, its operational procedures are from another era. Unquestionably, the blame for failure to modernize Selective Service falls on General Hershey, who has headed the system since 1941. He cannot admit that a system he created and administered with success during a time of great trial—World War II—is today an utter failure, an anachronism in a changed society.

At this point, we must concede some sympathy for General Hershey. For some twenty years, since the enactment of the peacetime draft, he has stubbornly tried to implement an impossible system. He has distorted the system, ignored its defects and fought off change. History is full of men unable to adapt to new situations. Long after the industrial revolution, old shoemakers could be found, toiling in their shops, turning out shoes no one wanted. Even as great an innovator as Thomas Edison, after inventing the electric light bulb, scoffed at the prospect of television. The inability to accept change or tear our minds from the accomplishments of yesterday may be a tragedy we are all destined to face one day. But it is unjust that an entire nation suffer needlessly because of the inflexibility of an elderly official.

Administratively, Selective Service is a shambles. Suppose when you went to buy an airline ticket the agent told you there would be a delay of three months to determine whether a seat was available on the flight. Through a national network of computers, the airlines can tell in seconds the space available on any flight. Selective Service makes no such concessions to progress. At any given moment, Selective Service doesn't know whether

two thirds of its 1-A pool is available for induction or not!
These men are lost in a bureaucratic maze known as the "pipeline."

On December 1, 1966, Selective Service had a 1-A manpower
pool (nineteen through twenty-five) of 934,365. Some 527,142
had not been examined (which is also the fault of the armed
services examining stations). Of the 407,223 who had been examined and qualified, only 133,824 were readily available for
induction. The other 273,399 were caught somewhere in the
pipeline; their papers were being shuffled back and forth between the local board and the examining stations or induction
centers or appeal boards, or just sitting around waiting for reclassification.[1] Sometimes it may take weeks for a boy's papers
to be processed. It's not unusual for boys awaiting examination
results to turn twenty-six and become ineligible for the draft.

Selective Service officials have no way of knowing whether the
1-A man they count on drafting has already enlisted. "We don't
find out that men have been recruited sometimes until sixty days
or so after they have been recruited," General Hershey told the
House Armed Services Committee. Thus, Selective Service is
issuing calls two or three months ahead of time on information
already three months old.

Because of the jam in the pipeline, Hershey maintains he
must have six men in the 1-A pool (examined and qualified) for
every one he inducts. Senator Jacob Javits of New York calls
this 6 to 1 ratio "a major cause of anxiety an uncertainty which
is wholly unwarranted. Six young men are kept apprehensive
about their futures so that one of them can be made available
for service."

Like many congressmen, Senator Javits suggests the obvious
solution: computers. "Just as many of our commercial airlines,
and indeed the military departments utilize massive computer
systems," says Javits, "each local board using remote data links
[to] Army examination centers and state directors can signifi-
cantly expedite availability and qualification data between state

directors and the national center. . . . In this age of computer technology, there is no excuse for manual processing of the 33 million registrants now on our manpower rolls." [2]

How does General Hershey react to suggestions of adjusting to the computer age? Negatively. He insists computers would destroy decentralization, "the heart and mind of the system," and eliminate the compassionate, individual judgments of local boards. "I am willing to put up with the mistakes of the local boards down there who can look into all the facts, and I have more confidence in them than I have in a computer," he said. The lack of serious attention paid to this subject during the House hearings is illustrated by the following dialogue between Chairman Rivers and Hershey:

> Rivers: Well now, General, this committee has no reason to have any peculiar affinity for or love for computers, we don't have any reason to recommend them. But do you think you could use any of these things, these data gadgets, in your organization?
>
> Hershey: Well, I have had three studies made by some of the Reserve Officers who are attached to us and I think their desires to make a sale would be greater than the fear of me, and they recommended that unless we wanted to change our decentralized system there wouldn't be much they could do for us."
>
> Rivers: I just wanted to be certain, because you see we got 200 million people in this country, and I was just throwing that out as a suggestion of improving the efficiency of the organization by taking advantage of modern technology from the headquarters down to the local boards, this is what I had in mind.
>
> Hershey: Well, I believe that we ought to use everything we can, but when we get into the sort of machinery that starts using us and that we begin to restrict what we can do because it won't go in the machine, then it bothers me not a little. You know we have a saying about the machine, that

it is just GIGO, garbage in—garbage out, and you will get
out of it just what you put in.[3]

Rivers: That is exactly right, precisely. A computer is no better
than the stuff you put in. It is like a deep freeze, if you
want a good steak, put a good steak in it. I would like to
have one. You are as right as you can be on that.

Computers and data-processing are used by small companies,
medium-sized companies and gigantic corporations—by the airlines, by the television industry, by hospitals, by colleges, by
General Motors, by the American Medical Association, by the
National Aeronautics and Space Administration (NASA), by the
Department of Defense and the Internal Revenue Service. It
seems that "these data gadgets" can be tailored to the requirements of nearly every organization in America except Selective
Service. General Hershey insists the special studies have determined that automatic data-processing is unworkable for Selective
Service. One would imagine the General had called in a team of
experts from IBM or Sperry Rand to make the surveys. But
Congressman Richard S. Schweiker of Pennsylvania was able to
obtain a copy of the most recent study so conclusively ruling out
data-processing. It was exactly three and a quarter typed pages
long; it was prepared by two Reserve colonels attached to Selective Service headquarters in April, 1965. Their entire study con-
sisted of re-examining two previous studies made in 1964 and
interviewing the staff at Selective Service headquarters!

Schweiker suggests a simple data-processing system in which
boards would fill out a punch card with a boy's name and classification and then send all the 1-A cards to a central staff data-
processing center, which would be hooked up with Selective
Service headquarters. "When a call came up for say, 30,000
men, a button could be pushed in national headquarters and you
would get a random selection of men from all over the country."

Hershey is opposed to Schweiker's plan—and others like it

that include a national manpower pool—because it would destroy another archaic Selective Service practice: draft quotas. After Selective Service receives a monthly call from the Department of Defense, it assigns a quota to each state on the basis of a formula.* State directors, in turn, apportion their quota among the local boards. The size of a state's quota depends not on the size of its male population (as many think it should) but on a criterion that is less fair, but more expedient for national headquarters. How many men a state must supply depends on the number of 1-A's it has immediately ready to go—available and qualified. In short, *not* in the pipeline. A state also gets credit for men already on active duty. This is to avoid penalizing a state that has heavy enlistments.

* The formula for computing the quota is:

The national call from the Secretary of Defense is allocated by the Director of Selective Service among the States on the basis of availability.

Availability for the United States and for each State is determined as follows:

The number of registrants nineteen to twenty-six who are classified as 1-A and 1-A-O who have not been examined or whose examination results have not been received is multiplied by the National or State (as appropriate) preinduction examination acceptance rate for the previous six months.

The product is then added to the number examined and qualified and that sum is multiplied by the appropriate induction examination acceptance rate of the preceding six months.

The product is an estimated availability for the Nation and each State.

The current outstanding call is deducted.

Then each State is given a quota which bears the same proportion to the national quota as the State's availability bears to the national availability.

Credits are accounted for in classification in that men in each State already inducted, enlisted or commissioned do not appear in the Total 1-A and 1-A-O reported.

It is obvious that this quota system will not distribute the burden of duty among all young men equitably. Quotas prohibit the nationwide enforcement of draft priorities. The President established priorities to insure an orderly, fair method of drafting men in turn. Assigning quotas defeats this purpose. In 1966, Alabama had to call up married men to satisfy quotas, while other states, such as Illinois, still had not exhausted their supply of single men. Some states were forced to dip into twenty-year-olds, while other states still had a plentiful supply of twenty-two-year-olds. Such inequities would be eliminated if we abolished quotas and simply drew draftees from one large national manpower pool of 1-A's. Each man would then be on an equal footing regardless of his state or home town. General Hershey objects to the chanciness of a draft lottery, but the current quota system creates no less a "chance by geography" situation.

Under the quota system, the boy with an inefficient draft board fares best. Although 1-A, he may still be at home, while his countrymen who live in states with more efficient draft boards may be on their way to Vietnam. Selective Service allocates its quotas on the basis of 1-A's whose papers have been completely processed and are, therefore, "available and qualified," ready for immediate induction. States with diligent, efficient draft boards that rapidly push registrants' papers through the pipeline have the most men available; as an ironic award for their competence, they are assigned larger draft quotas. States with boards that shuffle papers slowly are required to provide fewer boys.

In June, 1966, the Wednesday Club (a study group of 25 liberal Republican Congressmen) charged that Texas, because of inefficient boards, was "underdrafting," while states like Michigan, with efficient boards, were "overdrafting." The Republicans pointed out that Texas has 10,500,000 residents (5.4 per cent of the total population) and Michigan has 8,250,000 people (4.2 per cent of the population). Yet from July, 1964, through June 1966, Michigan's draft quota was 22,127; the quota for Texas was only 19,144. Michigan, with fewer people, was drafting 20 per cent more men.[4]

Texas Congressmen were incensed at what they took to be a slur on Texans' patriotism. Senator John Tower branded the charges of his Republican colleagues as "totally false." Colonel Morris Schwartz, director of Selective Service in Texas, countered by asserting that Texas' quota was lower because Texans were *more* patriotic; they had more credits for enlistments. He reported that as of March 31, 1966, enlistments for Texas totaled 102,130, compared with only 65,082 for Michigan. General Hershey, "clearing the matter up" before the House hearings in June, agreed that recruitment credits accounted for Texas' lower quota. Hershey's explanation was not questioned further. Some felt that the Wednesday Club had simply been mistaken.

This is unfortunate, for an examination of Selective Service's annual report of 1965 reveals that Michigan was not the only state forced to overdraft. Pennsylvania was suffering even more. Pennsylvania and Texas have almost exactly the same number of registrants of draft age. In fiscal 1965, Pennsylvania's quota was 7,306; the quota for Texas was a mere 3,881. Pennsylvania was obliged to supply *88 per cent more* draftees than Texas. In this case, Selective Service cannot brush aside the injustice by claiming that Texas had more enlistment credits. Pennsylvania had 124,026 men on active duty; Texas, only 97,736.

Such disparities are indeed linked to local board efficiency, as another part of the Selective Service annual report reveals. The overdrafting in Michigan and Pennsylvania is almost directly proportionate to the greater number of men they had processed through the pipeline to the point of being instantly available. Texas had only 12 per cent of its draft-age registrants examined and qualified; Michigan, 16 per cent, and Pennsylvania, 37 per cent. It is unfair to penalize efficient Selective Service operations by forcing them to sacrifice disproportionately high quotas of men. The old-fashioned quota system should be abolished. As

Congressman Schweiker says: "We have been the United States of America for some time, and Selective Service is the only department that doesn't recognize it."

A national manpower pool of 1-A's however, will not solve our entire problem. If we take only "examined and qualified" men from the national pool, efficient boards will still be punished. Ultimately, the pipeline must be cleared up. At the very least, an efficienty audit of local boards seems long overdue.

Many of the petty inequities of the draft can be traced to General Hershey's committment to decentralization. Under the decentralized system, the local board (usually three to five uncompensated citizens and one or more paid Civil Service clerks) acts independently, usually with only the most permissive guidance from national headquarters except in special cases when General Hershey steps in. Amazingly, *there are no firm national standards* which boards use to determine classifications, deferments or induction. Local boards are islands of autonomy. According to law, local boards are empowered "to hear and determine, subject to the right of appeal, all questions or claims with respect to inclusion for, or exemption or deferment from, training and service . . . of all individuals within the jurisdiction of such local boards."

Occasionally, Hershey's office sends out "guidelines" to local boards to give them direction. These guidelines are usually vague. During the Vietnam crisis, for example, General Hershey has advised local boards to defer only full-time college students. This sounds clear enough. But what constitutes a "full-time student"? Is it a boy taking twelve hours? Fourteen hours? Sixteen hours? When asked to define "part-time student" at the House hearings, General Hershey said he could not; he supposed a "part-time student" was one who would not graduate in four years. (This cannot be predicted: Suppose a boy taking twelve hours one semester takes nineteen the next?) He said it was impossible even to define "semester" and "trimester," because of differences among schools.

It seems inconceivable that Selective Service could not compile a directory of colleges with the stated number of hours each regards as "full-time." But whether it *can* be done is not the issue. The real obstacle here is General Hershey's adamant objection to national standards, ostensibly because he wants to leave the power at the "grass roots." When a Congressman suggested that local boards needed more specific guidelines, Hershey said: "They have more guidelines generally than they can read now."

In the absence of firm national criteria, boards are forced to make arbitrary decisions. Probably, once policy is established within a board, it is enforced with some consistency; but the policy itself may differ greatly from board to board. One board defers graduate students; another does not. As Congressman Schweiker says: "Presently we have as many different draft policies and standards as there are local draft boards—4,061 of them."

Boards given identical information about registrants may come to different conclusions. Three pilots in Pennsylvania, all holding identical jobs with the Flying Tiger Airlines, which carries cargo for the Department of Defense, applied for occupational deferments, claiming their essentiality to national defense. Two of the pilots were granted deferment by their boards. The third pilot, although more experienced than the other two, was denied deferment.

Similarly, the Department of Commerce wrote identical letters to two draft boards requesting deferment for two young college graduates working as management interns in the Department. One man received his 3-A occupational deferment; the other did not. Apparently, the deferred man was registered with a draft board in an urban, lower-middle-class area which had a plentiful supply of less well-educated, nondeferrable men from whom to pick its quota of draftees; the board was willing to spare the college graduate for public service. The man who was refused deferment was registered with a board in a prosperous middle-class community; to this board, a college graduate in the Commerce Department, when compared with dozens of other college men they had to consider, seemed nonessential. Two boards: identical information, opposite conclusions.

There can be no doubt that absence of national criteria creates a hodgepodge of inconsistencies and confusion. Chet Holifield, representative from California, virtually pleaded before the House Armed Services Committee in June, 1966, for, if not national standards, at least standards which would make draft policies uniform within a state. One could not blame him after hearing his woeful description of the messy state of affairs in California. Holifield said: "In one community, four boards are all operating out of the same building, but each independent of the other. As a consequence, each board has adopted its own procedures, its own practices and its own interpretation of the law and regulations. Some boards even have been further split into panels, again each with its own methods.

"The result is that one boy at a local college may be classified or drafted under one set of standards while his classmate and neighbor who lives across the street under a different board will be judged by different standards. One board decides to reclassify all college freshmen 1-A, while another defers them . . .

"We have in California some seventy-five junior colleges, with the curriculum containing the first two years of college, and the same standards as the four-year colleges. Yet, if a student attends a junior college—and this is where about 459,000 students, mostly poor students, are going to college—some boards are recognizing and respecting junior colleges; others do not.

"One board defers a student to the middle of October after registration, while another defers to the end of the school year in June. One board considers that a full-time student is one who takes thirty units of study, while another board requires twenty-four units; another says twelve." [5]

Such reports of glaring inconsistencies among local board decisions leave General Hershey unmoved. At the House hearings, after evidence of wildly variant board decisions had been presented, he was asked: "Now, again, do you believe there should be no more guidelines sent down to the local boards?" Hershey replied: "That is correct. That is correct."

General Hershey's opposition to uniform criteria is grounded in his belief that greater standardization will spoil the decentralization of the system. He expresses boundless faith in the autonomous decisions of local boards: "No system of compulsory service could long endure without the support of the people. . . . The Selective Service System, therefore, is founded upon the grassroots principle, in which boards made up of citizens in each community determine when registrants should be made available for military service."

A Selective Service bulletin further states: "Only a board composed of a man's neighbors having substantial information on national needs and thorough knowledge of his personal situation can achieve the maximum in individual and group fairness, justice and impartiality."

This is a fine sentiment, and it was probably valid in rural America circa 1917. But today's highly mobile urban society makes the "neighborhood" concept of local boards untenable.

In rural areas, there may still be community ties between board members and registrants, as Selective Service maintains. But in urban areas, contact with board members is nonexistent. In large cities like Chicago, the identity of board members is concealed to protect them from pressures and harrassment— and perhaps this is wise. But it is hypocritical to keep identities secret and then contend that boards make wise decisions because they know a boy's personal circumstances.

Theoretically, each county is supposed to have a local board. But in sparsely populated areas, one board may serve three or four counties; and in urban areas, a county has many boards to divide the workload. Cook County (Chicago and suburbs) for example, has 81 boards; their boundaries follow political wards as they existed in 1948.

A board member is required to reside in the county of his board's jurisdiction. But it is not mandatory that a board member live in his *district*. Said one professor: "What do the men who live on Chicago's plush North Shore in Cook County know of the circumstances of a Negro kid in Woodlawn?" In Philadelphia, charged one Congressman, some board members are never seen inside their district except on that one day a month when they drive up in their Cadillacs to pass judgment on the draftability of disadvantaged youngsters. The county, of course, is no longer a meaningful unit in American urban life, and draft boards can hardly be called representative cross sections of the community.

In the areas of Los Angeles where the Mexican-American population is concentrated, there are three draft boards. Only *one* draft board member is of Mexican-American descent. In the South, the "sympathetic neighbor" concept of local draft boards is a bitter joke. Negroes are drafted by all-white boards; in New Orleans, one board member also served as head of the local Ku Klux Klan. Allegedly, there are no Negroes at all on the boards of Arkansas, Mississippi and Alabama. The American Veterans Committee called this flagrant discrimination and pressed General Hershey to provide a racial breakdown of southern draft boards. He maintains that since 1948 Selective Service has not kept records that show board members' race. But when Congresswoman Edith Green of Oregon asked: "I would be curious to know, General Hershey, if Governor Wallace ever appointed a Negro in Alabama," Hershey replied: "I doubt it. I doubt if Alabama or two or three other states down there has a Negro on a local board."

In truth, General Hershey doesn't really know *what* kind of men are serving on local boards, although he calls them "the best people in the world." The only requirements are that a member be at least thirty years old, male, and reside in the county of his board's jurisdiction. Members, according to law, are appointed by the President upon the recommendation of the governor of each state. In actuality, the appointments are rubber-stamped all the way down the line. The governor usually chooses the man whom a retiring board member recommends to replace him. Then General Hershey automatically approves the governor's appointment in the name of the President.

Hershey makes no inquiry whatever into the man's qualifications. In remarking on his failure to make an independent review, Congressman William Fitts Ryan of New York said: "Let me repeat: General Hershey's top assistants can't remember a time when they ever rejected or scrutinized a man recommended by a state governor . . . Since these boards have so much discretionary power, I think it is fitting for this committee to inquire into who sits on them."

Board members serve without pay for indefinite terms. Many of them are retired businessmen, often veterans of World War I. Invariably, they are at least two generations removed from the boys they now send off to war. A national survey found that nearly half of all board members are over age sixty, and 20 per cent are over seventy. Recently, Selective Service announced the retirement of a board member aged ninety-four. Of the 16,000 board members, "hundreds," recounts General Hershey enthusiastically, "have served for twenty-five years or more. A few were on the boards in 1917."

The turnover among draft board members is negligible—a fact of which General Hershey is proud. To him, it proves their dedication. On the other hand, one Selective Service official complained that it is sometimes difficult to persuade an unsatisfactory member to resign. Appointments are made for an indefinite length of time, with no periodic dates for review. This led Arlo Tatum to suggest to the President's National Advisory Commission that local board appointments be for the length of the draft law itself (usually four years): "Even if reappointments were fairly automatic, it would give the system an opportunity not to reappoint members they found to be intransigent or unintelligent in their approach. In addition, there should be an automatic retirement age of say, seventy."

How many of the decisions do local board members actually make anyway? We are told that they pore over each case individually. This is pure fiction, an official deceit perpetuated to prop up General Hershey's insistence that the system is fair because every man, after all, is judged compassionately by his neighbors. As every registrant knows from experience, it is the local clerk who rules the board. She announces classifications, answers the telephone, keeps the files, replies to all correspondence and issues the Greetings. The local board meets once a month for three or four hours to ceremoniously validate what the clerk has decided. These sessions are largely ritualistic, except for the few cases in which the clerk can not decide herself and asks the opinion of the board.

As Congressman Holifield charged at the House hearings: "I want to emphasize that the Civil Service Commission clerks are running these boards, not the members. The members are men working without pay. They are doing a patriotic job . . . but I would say 85 per cent of the work of screening and classifying these boys is done by civil service clerks. Then when the board meets that night, they hand it to them, and they run through them and the clerk says 'This bunch on the top ought to go.' So they sign their names and they go. In many instances we are not achieving the principle that we thought we were achieving of having local businessmen and leaders in the community express evaluative judgment on the merits of specific cases. It is being done by low-pay grade clerks." [6]

John H. Hammack, state director of Selective Service in Illinois, denied that the clerks "have any say whatsoever in determining who will be drafted." He insists that clerks are forbidden to make recommendations except to explain bookkeeping procedures.

Such statements only make Selective Service look foolish. As Roger Little, associate professor of sociology at the University of Illinois, who did a study of Selective Services practices in Illinois in 1966, states: "It is obviously inconceivable that a board can actually individually consider the cases of 200 to 400 registrants in a single three-hour session and come to unanimous agreement on all of them."

Classifying, he confirms, is a routine administrative procedure, usually based on certain established criteria, and is performed by clerks. Professor Little does not regard this as objectionable, but as preferable. "The clerk is far more knowledgeable than the board members," he says. "She is the only expert in the board room when it meets." What is wrong, says Little, is that we pretend board members make the decisions when they don't. Little recommends that we legitimatize the clerk's function, by calling her a Registrar, and that we officially recognize the local boards as appeal boards only, which is what they are now.

Finally, Little says, "Preoccupation with such trivial issues as who sits on the board or whether the clerk really makes the decisions, is not as important as recognition of the fact that . . . the local board is obsolete. It had a real function for emergency manpower recruitment in a relatively rural society. But it is no longer a valid instrument in an urban society." [7]

7 ☆ General Hershey: Master Planner

"Peacetime conscription is the greatest step toward regimentation and militarism ever undertaken by the Congress of the United States."
—Senator Burton K. Wheeler, 1940.

After *Parade* magazine published in the summer of 1966 a reader's question asking "Is General Hershey head of the Hershey Chocolate Company in Pennsylvania?" an army officer, a long-time acquaintance of Hershey's, sent him the clipping with an attached note. It said, in effect, that the country would be much better off if Hershey were doing nothing more harmful than making chocolate drops. "He is an old friend," Hershey said, showing me the note, "but he thinks I am an evil man."

Lewis Blaine Hershey was born on a farm near Angola, Indiana, in 1893, and came up through the ranks of the Indiana National Guard, receiving a commission as an artillery captain in the regular Army in 1920. He became director of the Selective Service System in 1941. He is now one of the most powerful men in this country, responsible only to the President. He rules Selective Service—from his headquarters staff, down through state directors and local boards—with benevolent despotism. There are few Congressional laws to restrict his actions. Nearly all powers for procuring military manpower are discretionary with the President, who delegates the responsibility to the director of the draft. Specific Selective Service policies are made by Presidential regulations and memoranda to state directors and local boards. The memoranda, more properly called directives, require the approval of no one but General Hershey.

As a Congressional aide pointed out, "Hershey keeps his power by disclaiming it." He is eloquent in his deference to local boards: "Only a man's neighbors know all the circumstances to judge his case," and "They make the decisions, not I," he insists. Theoretically, local boards have complete autonomy. In reality, local board members and clerks rarely feel they are in a position to dispute the General's judgments. One call from Hershey can quickly reverse a board's decision. A young man recently was declared delinquent for failure to comply with draft board regulations, and according to established policy, was issued induction papers. The boy called his father who is president of a large university. The father called a dear friend, who is a Senator, who in turn gently suggested to General Hershey that "a mistake had been made." In three days, the boy had in his hands a cancellation of his orders. A mistake had been made, the board agreed.

Hershey will tell you that he doesn't make policy alone, that his decisions are tempered by consultations with other government agencies and national authorities. In truth, he makes draft policy almost single-handedly. In 1948, when the Trytten committees convened to decide student deferment procedure, Hershey opened the sessions by reminding them that the final authority lay with him, not them, and that they were "advisory" only. Thus, he let it be known that if he didn't like their recommendations, he wouldn't use them. Not surprisingly, the committees issued a report he could endorse.

When questioned by Carlton R. Sickles of Maryland during

the House hearings in February, 1966, Hershey, after insisting that he conferred with people in various departments of government before making decisions, could not name one he had conferred with. He did not know the route his proposed policies would take for circulation through government channels ("I'm sure the piece of paper does not wander around by itself," said Sickles) nor did Hershey know even a fact that is of monumental importance to all agencies: the name of his contact on the White House staff. Exasperated, Sickles pointed out the obvious, that Hershey is virtual draft-potentate, even to advising the President on specific policies. "Don't you see," demanded Sickles, "that even though the [draft regulations] are signed by the President, they are directives that are really *your* directives, and that you are making these decisions and that these are rather awesome decisions you are making?"

Few Americans comprehend the significance of the decisions General Hershey *is* making. In 1948, with the passage of the peacetime draft law, the General launched his vast deferment program to soak up the surplus of men. Simultaneously, the pragmatic General realized that deferments, like inductions, could be used extensively to promote the country's "health, safety and interest," and thus underwent his metamorphosis from mere military procurer to organizer of civilian manpower. Some citizens object to a suggested national service plan because it would give the draft a foot in the door to control over civilians. The worry is academic. The draft, some eighteen years ago, went through that door, albeit rather quietly and unnoticed. And the draft, once admitted to civilian life, immediately began to exercise its power.

Hopelessly out of date is the notion that the Selective Service System concerns itself primarily with inducting men, and that the consequences most of us view as evil—draft fear, anxiety and corruption of colleges—are unintentional. The major energies of Selective Service, by its own admission, go toward directing the lives of those millions of men who are *not* inducted.

The terrible uncertainty and draft fears that infuse young men's lives, which most citizens abhor and Congressmen seek to erase through reforms, are factors that Selective Service officials strive to retain in order to keep control over citizens. In 1940, Senator Robert A. Taft, bitterly opposing peacetime conscription, warned: "The compulsory draft is far more typical of totalitarian nations than of democratic nations. The theory behind it leads directly to totalitarianism." These were not idle words. We must face the fact that a quarter of a century later the draft as an instrument of terror is an American reality.

Proving that the government *intends* use of the draft for civilian control ordinarily would be impossible. We would be forced to merely speculate about motives—were it not for the existence of one of the most remarkable documents issued by a government agency. In a manifesto, innocuously titled "Channeling," dated July 1, 1965, Selective Service explicitly states that its primary purpose in the manipulation of deferments is control of the civilian population. This is not a secret paper; it is available to all who ask for it, but it is obvious that few reporters, Congressmen, or citizens have read or digested its contents.

"Channeling," as Selective Service defines it euphemistically, is "pressurized guidance," or use of the "deferment carrot," to force young men into certain occupations, jobs and activities that are "in the national interest." The psychological premise underlying channeling is age-old: That most men threatened by slavery prefer freedom, no matter how temporary or at what cost to human dignity. Hershey counts on the fact that a boy will do many things—take college courses, choose occupations, in fact change his life plans—to remain free. For channeling to be successful, the draft's authority must first have the power of universal male enslavement, which it does. It then must extend the promise of freedom to young men who will behave as directed. If they refuse, they are denied deferment. As long as a deferred man is under the threat of the draft, he is in debt to Selective Service—not unlike an ancient slave, granted *conditional* freedom by his master. It is by exploiting a boy's fear of losing his deferment and thus his freedom that General Hershey accomplishes "channeling" in the name of America's welfare.

The following excerpts are taken in order from the nine-page mimeographed Selective Service document, called "Channeling." The first sentence is an overall statement of purpose:

> One of the major products of the Selective Service classification process is the channeling of manpower into many endeavors, occupations and activities that are in the national interest.

We then discover that "procurement" has broader meaning than we ever dreamed; it can mean forcing men into *civilian* as well as military niches:

> The line dividing the primary function of armed forces manpower procurement from the process of channeling manpower into civilian support is often finely drawn. The process of channeling by not taking men from certain activities who are otherwise liable for service, or by giving deferment to qualified men in certain occupations, is actual procurement by inducement of manpower for civilian activities. . . .

Historically, channeling goes hand in hand with the extension of a wartime draft into peacetime.

> The opportunity to enhance the national well being by inducing more registrants to participate in fields which relate directly to the national interest came about as a consequence, soon after the close of the Korean episode, of the knowledge within the System that there was enough registrant personnel to allow stringent deferment practices employed during wartime to be relaxed or tightened as the situation might require.
>
> This was coupled with a growing public recognition that the complexities of future wars would diminish further the distinction between what constitutes military service in uniform and a comparable contribution to the national interest out of uniform. . . . The meaning of the word 'service' with its former

restricted application to the armed forces, is certain to become widened much more in the future.

In the next sentence, we receive the philosophy full-force.

This brings with it the ever increasing problem of how to control effectively the service of individuals who are not in the armed forces.

Selective Service solves this problem by granting liberal deferments—for example, in the field of science—to act as a "club to drive" individuals out of certain activities and into others.

No group deferments are permitted. Deferments are granted, however, in a realistic atmosphere so that the fullest effect of channeling will be felt, rather than be terminated by military service at too early a time.

In other words, Selective Service actively contrives to keep a man out of service until an older age so it can influence his life. Once a young man is in and out of the service, Selective Service's power over his choices is lost.

In this psychological climate, we are told, a "patriotic" person thrives:

He can obtain a sense of well being and satisfaction that he is doing as a civilian what will help his country most.

Young men who do not share General Hershey's designs for their future may suffer:

In the less patriotic and more selfish individual it engenders a sense of fear, uncertainty, and dissatisfaction which motivates him, nevertheless, in the same direction. He complains of the uncertainty which he must endure; he would like to be able to do as he pleases; he would appreciate a certain future with no prospect of military service or civilian contribution, but he complies with the needs of the national health, safety, or interest—or is denied deferment.

(He organizes his life to suit General Hershey, or he is drafted.)

The prose builds to a crescendo on the wonders of fear-inspired guidance.

> Throughout his career as a student, the pressure—the threat of loss of deferment—continues. It continues with equal intensity after graduation. His local board requires periodic reports to find out what he is up to. He is impelled to pursue his skill rather than embark upon some less important enterprise and is encouraged to apply his skill in an essential activity in the national interest.

(He works for the good of the state, and, under the threat of the draft, is not free to change his occupation or direction of his life, which is surely one of the glories of being a free man—the opportunity to admit mistakes and wrong choices and rectify them.)

> The loss of deferred status is the consequence for the individual who has acquired the skill and either does not use it or uses it in a nonessential activity.

> The psychology of granting wide choice under pressure to take action is the American or indirect way of achieving what is done by direction in foreign countries where choice is not permitted.

The name of the game is still totalitarianism, although the rules are different in this country.

Selective Service does not want a boy to discover too early that he is unqualified for service, or the fear-psychology to motivate him toward draft-goals will be useless.

> The earlier [rejection for service] occurs in a young man's life, the sooner the beneficial effects of pressured motivation by the Selective Service System are lost. . . . Once the label of 're-jectee' is upon him all efforts at guidance by persuasion are futile. If he attempts to enlist at seventeen or eighteen and is

rejected, then he receives virtually none of the impulsion the System is capable of giving him. If he makes no effort to enlist and as a result is not rejected until delivered for examination by the Selective Service System at about age twenty-three, he has felt some of the pressure, but thereafter is a free agent.

We learn next that establishing the 1-Y classification had a double purpose: It helped soak up the manpower surplus, and also transferred many men from 4-F to 1-Y, bringing them under the threat of induction, which "preserves some of the benefit of what we call channeling." Men who will probably never be inducted, nevertheless, are not allowed to escape to freedom of choice and peace of mind under 4-F, outside the draft's umbrella of control.

In American society, Selective Service tells us, absolute freedom to choose an occupation and guide your own life is impossible and should not be allowed:

> In the absence of [the draft] bright young men would be importuned with bounties and pirated like potential college football players until eventually a system of arbitration would have to be established. . . . From the individual's viewpoint, he is standing in a room which has been made uncomfortably warm. Several doors are open, but they all lead to various forms of recognized, patriotic service to the nation. Some accept the alternatives gladly—some with reluctance. The consequence is approximately the same.

In the final paragraph, Selective Service, imbued with enthusiasm over its greater mission, dismisses with contempt the notion that its energies are dissipated by such a minor task as supplying men to the military.

> Delivery of manpower for induction, the process of providing a few thousand men with transportation to an induction center, is not much of an administrative or financial challenge. It is in dealing with the other millions of registrants that the System is heavily occupied, developing more effective human beings in the national interest.

Thus, Selective Service indeed gives us an understanding of draft policies that otherwise would remain incomprehensible to ingenuous minds. A person who naïvely assumes the draft's main occupation is procuring men has a different vantage point from one who knows that broad student and occupational deferments—coupled with the draft's life-and-death threat—are flagrantly used to punish, reward and thereby coerce men into professions General Hershey believes are in the national good. In view of manpower needs, a student draft test is unnecessary. But in General Hershey's context it is not so foolish. It engenders the fear necessary to perpetuating his control. Fear, he also believes, encourages men to better develop their abilities, for example, by studying harder. "I've told everybody for the last three months: 'You people in school are going to see the best grades made this year that have been made in an awful long time,' " he said in January, 1966.

General Hershey is violently opposed to a lottery draft-system, as suggested by many, including Senator Edward Kennedy of Massachusetts. A lottery, Hershey admits, would wreck his "channeling" because deferments would be virtually eliminated. The Pentagon favors drafting younger men—at eighteen and nineteen; Hershey objects because with service completed young men would be free to conduct their lives without his "pressurized guidance." Senator Kennedy, and most citizens, want to eliminate draft-anxiety that paralyzes men's decisions, prevents them from finding jobs and drives some into occupations they dislike. In assuming that all sane men regard these as evils, we are mistaken. General Hershey regards such anxiety as a good that reminds men constantly that they "owe something to their country." Confronted with evidence that his social planning may have gone awry, and that boys are staying in college not out of dedication to country but for what the General calls "selfish aims," he becomes vindictive. This is exemplified by his treatment of men over twenty-six. In June, 1966, he favored drafting the over-age as a warning to boys who stay in college until twenty-six that they cannot escape. The armed forces did not want older men and, his wishes thwarted, he was reduced to merely threatening them by calling some of them in for examinations.

It is small wonder that we fail to comprehend decisions when they are made not on the basis of actual manpower needs, but on extraneous considerations of "channeling" of which we are not even aware.

We should not underestimate how seriously General Hershey takes his mission of "bettering the citizenry." During the House Armed Services Committee hearings in June, 1966, he declared his views often: "There isn't anything that can't be solved now by having an individual pursue the things you want him to pursue, and then use him . . . I think you are going to have to compel people to get better . . ."

Moreover, General Hershey believes that his "channeling" has been eminently successful. During the hearings, he testified: "I am convinced the policy of deferring students so far as possible had much to do with influencing students to enter school, to pursue studies diligently, and to practice the skills they acquired.

"From 1952-53 through 1963-64 the number of engineering degrees increased from about 27,000-28,000 annually to nearly 48,000 annually.

"There was a general increase in college entrance but the student of that eleven-year period was not born in years of high birth rates. He was born in the 1930's. I think the channeling effect of prospective deferment had much to do with the increased numbers.

"The increases were most significant in advanced degree fields. Over the period, masters and doctors degrees increased about threefold.

"From 1949-50 to 1961-62 the number of teachers increased from about 1,235,000 to about 1,984,000. In 1949-50 about 29 per cent of the teachers were men. In 1961-62 about 37 per cent were men. I know of no dramatic increase in pay or other attractions to account for this increase, especially among men. The teacher shortage was of national concern, particularly after Sputnik in 1957. But I believe that the fact that students know deferments for full-time satisfactory study were common, as well as for essential engineers and teachers, among others, had some influence on the general increases we have had in critical occupational areas.

"From 1951 through 1965, the nation produced over 100,-000 physicians, 46,000 dentists and 12,000 veterinarians.

"From July, 1950 through June, 1964 our graduate schools awarded 17,420 doctorates in the humanities. In 1950-51 the number was 975. In 1963-64 the number was 1,812." [1]

No one can measure exactly how much of the increase in college enrollment is due to the draft. Many complex social forces undoubtedly are at work, but it is certain that, as General Hershey says, the draft is a considerable influence on education and the economy. The nature of the influence, however, is a matter of dispute and concern. Trying to make over America—or any country—in your own image is a dangerous pastime. General Hershey, while trying to inculcate the values of his Hoosier background—hard work, self-sacrifice and conformity—has like most despots fallen into the major pitfall of social planning. He creates far more social evils than he erases.

Hershey's draft policies disrupt the economy, corrupt institutions of higher learning and distort the lives of young men, very often keeping them hidden, as Yale's President Kingman Brewster, Jr., says "in the endless catacombs of higher education." An Associated Press survey of businesses in June, 1966, found that industry was left short of college graduates, because young men were rushing into graduate school to avoid Vietnam service. The University of Maryland reported that applications for graduate school for the fall of 1966 numbered 15,000, more than double the 7,000 for the fall of 1965. George Washington University in 1966 had a 30 per cent rise in graduate applications and New York University graduate applications were up 18 per cent over those of the previous year. Officials at all three universities attributed the rise to fear of the draft.

Students in the sciences are almost always given top-priority deferment. So many boys have been "channeled" into engineering, mathematics and the physical sciences that, according to the February, 1966 issue of *Science* magazine, we may soon have an excess. "The production of degrees—bachelor's, master's and doctor's—has been mounting faster than expected," they report. For example, in 1962, scientists had set a goal of 30,000 master's degrees in the three fields for 1970. They now expect to exceed that goal by 8,000. *Science* says that the scientific fields may become so glutted that colleges may have to cut back in these areas and become more selective in their science students.

Congressman Curtis reported in the Congressional Record in July, 1966, that General Hershey was not using up-to-date information in his "channeling." Selective Service determines which skills are essential and critical according to a publication titled "U.S. Department of Commerce List of Currently Essential Activities/U.S. Department of Labor List of Currently Critical Occupations." Local boards refer to this list in deciding whom to defer. The list currently used was published in December, 1963, and the occupations in the list are described in terms of the *Dictionary of Occupational Titles,* published in 1949, and its supplement, dated 1955, although a new dictionary was published in 1965.[2]

Perhaps the greatest tragedy of channeling is the corruption of a boy's occupational and educational plans. Several law students at the Berkeley campus of the University of California said: "We don't intend to be lawyers. We just want to stay out of the draft. It was a choice of taking law or teaching." A boy at the University of Texas said he would like to go into real estate, but was afraid the draft would take him. "I guess I'll study sociology until the war is over." A Stanford senior in the school of education confessed: "I hate teaching."

In a statement before the Senate Subcommittee on Employ-ment and Manpower in 1963, John C. Esty, Jr., former associate dean at Amherst and now headmaster of the Taft School, con-firmed that more and more young men make their life-decisions under the influence of the draft. "In about ten years of counsel-ing college students on military service, I have seen this effect first-hand. A student chooses his major field because it leads to a job in an essential industry. A senior plans to keep his student deferment by continuing on to graduate school even though it makes no sense educationally. A career field is chosen arbitrar-ily just because it will mean an automatic deferment. Some stu-dents are paralyzed for effective planning of their lives because they can't figure out where the draft fits in. . . . It strikes me as ironic that with all the current concern over federal control of education and interstate eating places, Selective Service may well exert a far more invidious and subtle form of control than we have ever suspected." [3]

Hershey holds the honorary degree of Doctor of Laws from eight colleges and universities. In one light this is excessive rec-ognition. In another, it is undue compensation for the vast amount of work General Hershey does for our institutions of higher learning. His capacities include registrar, admissions offi-cer, dean of counseling, guidance counselor, disciplinarian, test-ing and grading advisor, job placement officer and professor of psychology. General Hershey, in carrying out his channeling sys-tem, does not shrink from opportunities to exercise his power. Many boys who believe they are the innocent victims of a sys-tem they don't understand are in fact the sacrifices to a social scheme they don't know exists. Just as he uses the 2-S to push men into college, he withdraws it to push them out if their edu-cational plans do not conform to his preconceptions.

In June, 1966, a young man graduated from Pennsylvania State University with a bachelor of arts degree, a B-minus aver-age and long-time plans to go on to medical school to study podiatry. He was accepted at the Pennsylvania College of Podiatry for the following fall, received above 80 on the college deferment test, which was supposed to indicate to draft boards that he was qualified for graduate work. During the summer, the boy suddenly found himself reclassified 1-A and served induction papers. He appealed the decision to his district appeal board and they concurred by a vote of two to one that the young man deserved a 2-S. To them he was a serious, capable student and his pursuit of podiatry came under the "healing arts" which entitled the boy, like any other medical student, to deferment. The boy, regaining his student status, was considerably relieved.

But the district appeals board decision was at variance with General Hershey's wishes. The Pennsylvania State Director of Selective Service, Brigadier General Henry M. Gross, allegedly at General Hershey's request, took it upon himself to forward the boy's file to Selective Service's national headquarters so Hershey could present the case to a Presidential Appeal Board, he hoped for a reversal of the decision. A state director can legally do this if he believes that the local appeal board decision has been so far afield as to be injurious to the whole Selective Service System. Since this is a weighty claim, the regulations, section 1627.1, demands there must be cause. "Before he forwards a registrant's file to the director of Selective Service, the state director of Selective Service shall place in such file a written statement of his reasons for taking such appeal." Pennsylvania's state director Gross complied, so to speak. At least he wrote a letter dated September 1, 1966. It read: "I am appealing this case to the Presidential Board to insure full appellate review prior to further processing." The reason clearly is, he is appealing because he is appealing.

The Pennsylvania boy had, as most aspiring podiatrists do, completed four years of undergraduate work, as a prerequisite for graduate school. The President of the Pennsylvania College of Podiatry says that 80 per cent of their students have baccalaureate degrees, that the applications far exceed the acceptances, and that the boy most likely would not have been admitted without the B.A. degree. As a matter of policy, however, the college, like most podiatry colleges, states in its catalogue that two years of college is a minimum requirement. General Hershey believes, despite current practice, that two years of undergraduate work is adequate for podiatrists. In a letter he explained that the boy's deferment was brought to Presidential appeal because "his educational background exceeds considerably the minimum requirements for entrance into a college of podiatry." At this writing, the boy's case has not been decided, but whether he is granted or denied a 2-S, the implications of Hershey's power remain the same. Is a boy who wants to be a podiatrist to be denied a liberal arts education just because General Hershey calls it "excess education"? Is the *minimum* educational requirement all that should be honored? Should schools be forced to set their entrance standards to conform to General Hershey's dictates? Through deferment withdrawals, he can compel colleges to accept certain boys and penalize others who want knowledge beyond what Hershey decrees. Indirectly, Hershey has the power to set admission standards of any college in the country.

In the fall of 1965, another boy began college, but found it too expensive. In January he quit and worked until the following August to earn enough money to continue his education. He then enrolled at St. Benedict's College in Kansas where he achieved an average of 2.85 out of a possible 4 points. He took the draft test, passed, and felt relatively certain he would be back on campus in the fall. In the summer of 1966, he was suddenly reclassified 1-A. When he objected, he received little sympathy from the clerk at the draft board. "I was a bit disconcerted by her attitude," explained the boy. "She as much as said 'It's your tough luck for transferring.' " The boy appealed the 1-A classification, and the dean of his college recommended that the boy be returned to 2-S status. But the appeal was denied, and the boy was allowed only to finish one semester in 1966.

The manhandling of this youngster by Selective Service makes a mockery of the American dream that everyone, no matter how poor, can escape the log cabin through diligence and education. One would think that General Hershey would be especially sympathetic to this ambition. But the boy was yanked out of school because in a written verdict by General Hershey, "he is not making normal progress in his educational process in that it will take him approximately four and a half years rather than four years to complete his undergraduate education." In the view of General Hershey it is a crime punishable by draft and possible death to take one semester out of college—because it is not "normal." Some educators often recommend that troubled boys take time off from college to travel, work, find themselves, mature. But that is no longer possible under the Hershey regime, unless the maturing process includes a trip to boot camp. Young men must goose-step it straight through four years. There is no place for the boy who must interrupt his schooling to earn money for tuition, or for the part-time student. Boys must arrive on the campus in September assured of the $1,500 to $3,000 to see them through the year.

Such a policy, besides being educationally destructive and morally indefensible, establishes class privilege on the campuses more firmly and discriminates in a most unAmerican way against poor boys seeking to better themselves. Such are the consequences of social planning by amateurs. It is a national outrage that the colleges, the very bastion of academic freedom where young men are supposed to be free to pursue knowledge, have come under the dictatorial powers of Selective Service.

There is no reason to believe that General Hershey is less than passionately sincere in his desire to better his country and its citizens. He surely did not come to the job with any grand scheme of national domination. If the general usurped power, it was because we left it around for him to usurp. His "channeling" philosophy was undoubtedly conceived to fill a vacuum. When millions of boys had to be deferred anyway, why not manipulate deferments for a national purpose? It would not be like the pragmatic, zealous general to let such an opportunity to mold young men's characters for "the good of the country," go unexploited.

Nevertheless, General Hershey's power to terrorize and dominate a civilian population must be terminated. It is highly doubtful that a referendum of the American people would leave such power in his hands. In 1965, Congress refused appropriations for a modest Defense Department proposal, called STEP, to educate and rehabilitate 40,000 rejected men who wanted to enlist in the Army. Congressmen deemed such education outside the proper scope of the military. (The following year, McNamara undertook a similar program without extra funds). Is it likely that Congress then would sanction as a proper function of Selective Service the character-building and "pressurized guidance" of 30 million men who are not even in the armed forces?

We can only speculate that Congress, as much as the American people, would be shocked by the totalitarian philosophy and misused power of Selective Service, if it were brought to their attention. The issue has not been debated in Congress. In April, 1964, John Lindsay, then in the House, attempted to alert Congress to the insidious effects of the draft. He said: "Compulsory military training allows the federal government consciously to exert an influence over the individual's choice of profession or occupation. The military tends to influence young men into jobs that relate to the cold war, that enhance the position of the military in society. One way this is done is by deferments from the draft. General Hershey last year remarked that 'the deferment is that carrot that we have used to try to get individuals into occupations and professions that are said by those in charge of Government to be the necessary ones.' Deferments, then, are extended to nuclear scientists, but not to classicists, sociologists or political scientists, who, says the Government, are less essential to national security. Thus, in the name of 'national security' and 'government interest' the future course of emphasis in our society may be changed by the state, indeed by the military apparatus." [4]

Lindsay's voice, along with those of fifteen other Republican Congressmen seeking draft reform, was quickly muted by a Presidential announcement of a new draft study—the famous Pentagon study that is still suppressed. Lindsay's statement, as forceful as it was, lacked the detailed proof of Selective Service intent that the "channeling" paper now provides. Congress must soon decide how much longer America must endure General Hershey in the position he has so quietly assumed: minister of fear and control over free citizens.

8 ☆ Persecution of Dissenters

> *"We have gone way hog wild on individual
> rights in this country."*
> —Lieutenant General Lewis B. Hershey

On October 15, 1965, thirty-nine demonstrators, all but one of
whom were teachers or students at the University of Michigan,
protested against the war in Vietnam by holding a sit-in at a
local Ann Arbor draft board office. Reportedly, the students sat
quietly in a waiting room while the clerks went about their business as usual. "They didn't make any trouble for me," said one
clerk. When the offices closed at about six o'clock, the students
refused to leave. The police came, at which point a few students
went limp and had to be carried out; the others walked to the
patrol wagons. All were arrested, found guilty of trespassing and
were fined or sentenced to ten days in jail. Most of the protesters
appealed their convictions, and it was assumed that the matter
had come to rest where it belonged—in our court system.

But the Selective Service System decided to enforce a peculiar
justice of its own. Colonel Arthur Holmes, Michigan's Selective
Service director, was incensed to discover that many of the pro-

testers possessed student deferments. Retaliation was swift. He instructed local boards to send him the files of all demonstrators registered in Michigan. He also spread the alarm nationwide. After calling General Hershey's office for approval, Holmes sent letters to the Selective Service directors of the states where the boys were registered, claiming they had interfered with the operation of the Ann Arbor board. Holmes suggested the young men had violated a Selective Service law, and could be relieved of their 2-S deferment.

One by one the demonstrators felt the wrath of the draft. They were reclassified 1-A. Finally, 15 of the Ann Arbor protesters—from Michigan, Illinois, Washington, D.C., and New York—had lost their deferments and stood vulnerable to induction. Some were declared "delinquent," meaning they would be drafted immediately under the priorities, before all other 1-A's registered with their boards. In reclassifying the boys, Selective Service officials did not hide their motives. The Washington, D.C., board readily admitted their registrant in question had been reclassified 1-A because of participation in the sit-in. A New York board spelled out the reason in one protester's delinquency notice. Colonel Holmes called for the "immediate induction" of demonstrators who "interfere with the draft." And the Illinois Selective Service director as much as said that colleges which didn't approve of student demonstrators should let him know and he would have them inducted.

General Hershey told the University of Michigan's campus newspaper: "I'm one of those old-fashioned fathers who never let pity interfere with a spanking."

The general was, as Congressman Emanuel Celler of New York charged, using the Selective Service law as a "club to discourage and prevent political dissent." General Hershey did not approve of these boys' actions, and he undertook to punish them publicly. To the general with his notable insensitivity to individual rights and his strict insistence on duty to the state, reclassifying the students was not improper. In the general's mind, draft-eligible boys are allowed to remain in college through the generosity of Selective Service. They are not really free agents. As the General puts it: they are "on parole."

Hershey is convinced that boys of the type who demonstrate against the country's foreign policy by "breaking laws" will not make good citizens anyway. Deferring them, therefore, is no longer in the "national interest." Said Hershey of the Ann Arbor demonstrators: "They have violated the terms of their parole, and they have no business to have a deferment after that. I cannot think that they qualify under national health, safety or interest. . . . We made a mistake when we put [them] in this deferred classification and therefore I think [they] ought to be taken out."

Americans generally, including Congressmen, the press and the courts, have treated Selective Service with unusual gentleness. But its action in Ann Arbor was too offensive to be overlooked. Senator Philip A. Hart of Michigan, in a speech on the University of Michigan campus, sized up the horrible implications of the students' punishment, as not only an injustice to the boys, but as a warning to other deferred students that opinions unpopular with the state would not be tolerated. Said Hart: "The silencing effect of the reclassification is the real threat to freedom. It is this we must protest. The pressure on other students who now have deferments to refrain from expressing their views because of fear of reclassification is where the real danger lies. . . . The clearly implied intent, or at least the result, of the reclassifications was to say to students across the nation: 'Let this be a lesson to you.' " [1]

Indeed, General Hershey bragged that the reclassifications had been effective. He explained in the *Washington Post,* December 15, 1965: "Reclassification is quicker at stopping sit-ins than some indictment that takes effect six months later. And we haven't heard of any sit-ins since the one in Ann Arbor." The *Post* retorted editorially: "Induction into the armed forces ought not to depend on conformity to General Hershey's standards of political orthodoxy. The general has done something much worse than an injustice to an individual. He has impaired confidence in the fairness of the draft. And he has threatened a fundamental American freedom—freedom of expression." A few weeks later, the *Post* declared that if General Hershey could not be "persuaded" to instruct boards to stop using the draft law to stifle expressions of opinion, "he ought to be replaced with a director who will do so." Many others, including a group of 108 professors of law, the American Veterans Committee, and the American Jewish Congress, called for Hershey's dismissal. It is said that even the White House was irritated by Hershey's heavy-handedness.

From all indications, General Hershey was surprised and not a little confused by the intensity of the attacks. He was pushed to defend himself, and in so doing, became entangled in a rigamarole of contradictions from which there was no escape. Part of the time he maintained that the boys were reclassified because they were "delinquent" under draft regulations (1642.4). But, as M. H. Trytten pointed out in the House hearings of the Subcommittee on Education in February, 1966, delinquency had no relevance in the Ann Arbor case. "After looking over the regulations," said Trytten, "I find that delinquency is a technical term as far as Selective Service is concerned; it is defined as a failure to do something, such as failure to register, or to keep the board informed as to where the individual is . . . All of these are acts of *omission* [that] permit reclassifying as 1-A."

Other times General Hershey insisted that the boys were reclassified because they broke a Selective Service law, presumably section 12(a), which states that "any person or persons who shall knowingly hinder or interfere or attempt to do so in any way, by force or violence or otherwise, with the administration of this title or the rules or regulations made pursuant thereto," can be punished with five years imprisonment and/or a fine of $10,000.

However, if this were the case, as all Americans know, the

boys must be tried in a court of law. Selective Service cannot act as accuser, judge and jury, find the boys guilty and sentence them to two years in the Army. But this is exactly what the draft boards, with General Hershey's approval, attempted to do. The general's utter failure to comprehend the outrage he committed was evident in his statement to the *Detroit News* on December 19, 1966: "I contend this is a violation of our law and we do not have to go to court to find it out." Hershey maintained he was honoring the wishes of Congress by drafting the offenders, rather than "letting them go to prison."

For an uncomfortably long time, it appeared that the verdict of the draft boards would be allowed to stand. Some boards did relent and restored the 2-S to their registrants; but eight of the demonstrators remained 1-A. Six of the students chose to carry their case through the Selective Service appeal procedure. Unknown to most Americans, the Selective Service has an appellate system composed of one appeal board in every federal court district and a "final" Presidential Appeal Board of three members. Any resemblance between the draft's appellate system and our judicial appellate system, as implied by the nomenclature, is transparently false.

Before officially contacting the district appeal board, a boy can request a personal appearance before local board members to try to persuade them to change their minds. *He cannot be represented by a lawyer;* this is expressly forbidden by Selective Service regulations, although the prohibition, says the American Civil Liberties Union, is a clear violation of the constitutional right to counsel. One of the University of Michigan boys was granted a personal appearance of five minutes by his Illinois board, while his lawyer was forced to wait in the anteroom.

If the board denies the boy's claim, he can, within ten days, file an appeal with the district appeal board. The boy himself cannot appear before the appeal board. His case must be presented in writing only; he has no chance whatever to refute the arguments against him. He never learns why his appeal was granted or rejected (the boards do not issue written opinions). If he loses at the state level, he does not have an automatic appeal to the Presidential Board. He has the right to Presidential appeal only if the district board's decision was split. It is also possible for Selective Service state directors and the national director personally to intervene and ask for Presidential appeal.

Ostensibly, the appeal system exists to iron out injustices meted out by local boards. In effect, the appeal boards rubber-stamp local board decisions to such an extent that Selective Service notes with pride: "The small percentage of disagreement between local board classifications and those of boards of appeal and of the Presidential Appeal Board . . . bespeaks the fundamental soundness of local board actions." A district appeal board in California, for example, in 1964-65 upheld 86 per cent of the local board decisions.

Appealing is usually frustrating and futile—as the six students from Ann Arbor found out. In September, 1966, the Presidential Appeal Board of Selective Service handed down its not surprising decision. The draft protesters at Ann Arbor were guilty as charged by the local boards, by Colonel Holmes and General Hershey. The 1-A reclassification was justified, the board decreed. Thus did Selective Service try and convict six young men in absentia for expressing political opinions disagreeable to the state.

Ordinarily, if a boy is turned down by the national Selective Service appeal board, he is at a dead end. Lawyers in the past have found it nearly impossible to transfer a boy's case from the Selective Service's mock judicial system to our legitimate courts of law. The only way for a boy to get his case into a legally constituted court was to refuse induction, thus committing a criminal act, for which he may be punished by five years in prison and/or a $10,000 fine. Understandably, few boys are willing to take this risk. A man who breaks a traffic law, steals from his employer, commits rape or murder, can get a fair and open hearing in court, with the benefit of legal counsel. But a boy who offends the Selective Service System cannot.

If the courts were to review draft classifications before induction on a wide scale, especially in wartime, as one lawyer put it: "military conscription could be brought to a halt by thousands of suits challenging classifications." Thus, the courts have been extremely reluctant to risk damaging the efficiency of Selective Service by interefering in its operation. In the Ann Arbor case, however, General Hershey overstepped his jurisdiction so far that a federal court felt compelled to respond to the draft's attempts to take the law into their own hands and to suppress free speech. A federal court can agree to hear any case involving a denial of constitutional rights. Thus, two of the Ann Arbor demonstrators—29-year-old Peter Wolff and 22-year-old Richard Shortt—went directly to the courts, instead of trying to fight their case through the Selective Service System. The two were granted a hearing by the Second Circuit Court of Appeals in New York on the basis that the issue of free speech was of greater import than the normal non-interference policy regarding Selective Service.

In a precedent-setting decision, issued January 30, 1967, the court unanimously held that Selective Service had exceeded its jurisdiction (because "these two students have never been indicted or tried or convicted of this offense in a district court") and had violated the First Amendment guaranteeing free speech. "It is not the function of local boards in the Selective Service System to punish these registrants by reclassifying them 1-A because they protested as they did over the government's involvement in Vietnam," said the judges. They noted also that "attempts to secure relief within the Selective Service System itself would be futile," since draft officials had consistently maintained that the 1-A reclassifications were justified.

After stating that the court was "always most reluctant to bring any phase of Selective Service under judicial scrutiny," the judges agreed: "Only the most weighty consideration could induce us to depart from this long-standing policy. But of all constitutional rights, the freedoms of speech and assembly are the most perishable, yet the most vital to the preservation of American democracy. . . . Thus, the allegations of the complaint in this case that the draft boards have unlawfully suppressed criticism must take precedence over the policy of nonintervention in the affairs of Selective Service." [2]

Lawyers, according to the American Civil Liberties Union, consider this a "landmark" decision, for it opens the way for a judicial review of other Selective Service practices that violate individual rights.

With the Vietnam war, the government, as one Senator observed, has reached "near hysteria" in its efforts to discourage young men's opposition to the draft. The pinnacle of absurdity in this campaign is the petty draft-card burning law pushed through Congress in August, 1965, by L. Mendel Rivers. During the trial of the first offender, New Yorker David Miller, who publicly burned his draft card in an anti-war rally in Manhattan, the judge remarked to the defense attorney: "It might be that you and I could agree that this is not an earthshakingly important law."

It is probable that most of us also would agree that there is nothing damaging to the operation of Selective Service in burning a draft card. The distinguished educator Robert Hutchins commented: "Destroying the card does not affect the obligation to service: it is a demonstration, and demonstration is protected by the First Amendment. There is no doubt that the framers of the law against the destruction of cards did so with the deliberate purpose of suppressing this form of free speech." Indeed the Justice Department does not consider the destruction of the card itself an offense. So far, about nine boys who have burned their draft cards in anti-war protests have been arrested. A young man in Iowa who destroyed his draft card in protest because the Army would not let him enlist was not arrested. The law is selectively enforced, depending on which side of the foreign policy fence you are on.

Since Vietnam, government officials have also embarked on a vigorous, unwarranted persecution of young men seeking conscientious objector (CO) status. One obstacle to justice is that local boards have little understanding of the law governing conscientious objection, and Hershey's office makes little effort to enlighten them. In 1948 a pet philosophy of General Hershey's was inserted into the law, insisting that a conscientious objector's religious feeling be defined by his "belief in relation to a Supreme Being." Not surprisingly draft officials interpreted this as a traditional belief in God. But in 1965, the Supreme Court redefined "Supreme Being," ruling that a conscientious objector did not have to profess belief in God in the conventional sense. In the *U.S. v. Seeger* decision, the Court ruled:

> We have concluded that Congress, in using the expression 'Supreme Being' rather than the designation 'God' was merely clarifying the meaning of religious training and belief so as to embrace all religions and to exclude essentially political, sociological or philosophical views. We believe that under this construction, the test of belief 'in relation to a Supreme Being' is whether a given belief that is sincere and meaningful occupies a place in the life of its possessor parallel to that filled by the orthodox belief in God of one who clearly qualifies for exemption.

This "parallel religious belief" could be love, truth, justice, goodness and so forth.

Not only do local boards have difficulty interpreting this sophisticated concept, but many claim never to have heard of the decisions. And the change in the law can not be discovered by reading the CO application form, for General Hershey's office has staunchly refused to update the "Supreme Being" question on the form to conform with the Supreme Court decision. Hence, many boards go along rejecting boys for the same old reason: "Well, he said he didn't believe in God, didn't he?"

Selective Service should be obliged to inform registrants of their legal rights to conscientious objector status; instead draft officials often frustrate the dissemination of information. The director of Selective Service in Vermont absolutely forbade the posting of information explaining CO provisions of the draft law in local board offices. The government also harasses agencies that technically are performing services that Selective Service should be performing. For example, the telephone wires of the Central Committee for Conscientious Objectors in Philadelphia, which counsels boys, are allegedly tapped.

If a registrant is denied CO status by his local board, and then appeals, his claim goes to the Justice Department for a decision. After an FBI investigation the young man presents his case to a hearing officer, who is often a lawyer or a judge. The hearing officer makes a recommendation to T. Oscar Smith, chief of the Conscientious Objector Section of the Non-Criminal Division of the Department of Justice. Smith then forwards his "recommendation" to the district appeal board which usually regards Smith's decision as mandatory. Smith is famous for his "Road to Damascus" letters, which he has been turning out recently with increased zeal. In these letters, Smith subtly expresses his suspicion that the young man has suddenly experienced a religious conversion to escape the draft. "Sudden accessions of religious belief may be utterly sincere as the memorable one on Damascus Road, but they seldom synchronize perfectly with external facts making them convenient," is Smith's well-known prelude to a denial of CO status because of "insincerity."

Ordinarily, the Justice Department's Smith grants far more CO claims than he turns down. Prior to the escalation of the war, about 85 per cent of Smith's recommendations that came across the desk of Arlo Tatum, of the Central Committee for Conscientious Objectors, were favorable. Today Smith is approving only 5 per cent of the claims Tatum sees, and rejecting 95 per cent, mostly on the grounds of "insincerity." Tatum said that during three months (November, 1966, to January, 1967) Smith had accepted only *one* out of 21 applications for conscientious objector status—an unprecedented record. "Before this I had never had two unfavorable recommendations cross my desk in succession," said Tatum. "Now we get fifteen negative decisions in a row." During the three months, Smith even reversed four favorable recommendations from hearing officers, which again is highly unusual and irregular.

To justify the rejection of one recent CO applicant, Smith was obliged to distort the information on the FBI investigative report to such an extent that a prominent minister in New York City sent him a letter of protest, after the minister saw how his characterization of the boy had been twisted to support Smith's decision. In December, Smith rejected a boy, who had been religiously active for several years and from all indications was sincere, partly on the grounds that one of his co-workers had labeled him "a loudmouth" and "discourteous." As the young man's attorney (the decision is being appealed in a federal court) noted, such justification is far beyond the scope of the law, for "there is nothing in the statutes that says a conscientious objector must be of pleasant temperament and courteous to all persons."

General Hershey's office too has reversed its policy on conscientious objection. Some young men allow themselves to be inducted and then discover that they cannot conscientiously participate in military activity. Usually, there is no dishonor attached to such a situation. The man applies for a discharge as a conscientious objector or requests transfer to noncombatant duty. The request for CO status is sent by the military to General Hershey's office for an advisory opinion, which is faithfully followed. Prior to Vietnam, Hershey approved 80 per cent of the applications. In 1963, he gave favorable decisions in 116 out of 143 cases. At present General Hershey is approving only 4 per cent of the requests, and these appear to be cases in which the military wants an excuse to discharge the man for administrative reasons.[3] The man's beliefs, his sincerity, and his answers to questions on the application are inconsequential when the draft automatically stamps each application NO. This is not justice, but capricious enforcement of the law that discriminates against young men whose convictions have taken root during a time of inconvenience to the government.

Reportedly, government officials are refusing conscientious objector claims because they believe boys are objecting to the Vietnam war in particular instead of to *all* war in general. Under the law, only pacifists can quality for conscientious objector status; they must oppose "war in any form." It is certainly true that many boys seeking conscientious objector classifications actively oppose the war in Vietnam. But to deny their CO claims on this basis is twisted logic indeed—for if they are against all war, they perforce *must* object to Vietnam. Logically—if the draft's decisions were made on logic—a fierce opposition to Vietnam should bolster a boy's case for CO status rather than damage it.

Relative to the question of conscientious objection and the Vietnam war, we should re-examine the basis of the conscientious objector law. Why is CO status granted only to pacifists? The pacifist position—opposition to *all* war *per se*—is a comparatively radical religious concept. The pacifist provision was inserted in the law in 1917 to accommodate the beliefs of religious sects, such as the Quakers and Mennonites—many of whom fled to this country to escape the conscription and militarism of Europe. (It is ironic to note that General Hershey's own ancestors, who were Mennonites, were among the refugees from conscription.)

However, a much older religious doctrine, concerning the obligation to fight in war, is completely ignored by Selective Service. It is the "just war" theory, deeply rooted in Catholic theology, and defined by Saint Augustine some 1,600 years ago. Under this concept, not all wars are equally justified; the justice of a particular war can be evaluated. This philosophy seems to present an eminently more sensible approach. For, just as few men will say, "I'm for *all* wars," few can say, "I'm opposed to all wars." There are even pacifists who believe that conquering Hitler was a just and vital cause in the preservation of freedom. Surely it is true that many boys who cannot find it in their consciences to fight in Vietnam would fight to the end to defend their homes and their country if America were invaded. Many religious leaders urge that the conscientious objector provisions be expanded to incorporate the "just war" approach to military service. This would provide the usual conscientious objector alternatives—complete nonparticipation, alternative service in a civilian project or noncombatant duty within the services—to men who find killing in Vietnam conscientiously unbearable.

Quite often the initial reaction to a plea of tolerance for boys who cannot conscientiously fight in Vietnam is: "What has the country come to when young men can pick and choose their wars?" Somehow many Americans believe that if anyone who wanted conscientious objector status were to receive it, our youth would desert in droves. This is an ill-founded fear and reflects a misunderstanding of our youth and a certain lack of confidence in our foreign policy. It cannot be said that Americans have failed to respond to a call to arms, nor is there reason to think that many youth today would refuse to serve, although admittedly the war in Vietnam cannot be called one of our more popular wars. Few youths at any time are willing to take on the stigma attached to conscientious objection or to resist the authority of an institution as powerful as the United States government.

Said Richard E. Rubenstein, a Washington attorney, recently: "The vast majority of America's young men have always been conformist in useful ways. They prefer to go where the action is, to be with their colleagues, even in war, rather than be banished from that company. And as Vietnam demonstrates daily, Americans make willing, brave and skillful soldiers.

"Defense Department officials would probably be the first to admit that if an announcement were made tomorrow at Danang Air Base offering to transfer out any man who had lost faith in the American cause and who was prepared to explain his views to a hearing board, there would be few—if any—takers." [4]

The Scandinavian countries (Denmark, Sweden, Norway and Finland) grant conscientious objector status to anyone who as proof of sincerity will serve alternative civilian service for a longer time than is required for military duty. England, too, before it abolished conscription in 1960 had even more liberal provisions for conscientious objectors. (Some men, regardless of the reason for their objection, did not even have to perform alternative service.) In these countries only about 2 per cent of the young men requested CO exemption from military duty. This is slightly higher than our present ratio, but hardly enough to be damaging. Some individuals and groups suggest adoption of the Scandinavian policy in America, as the only safeguard for all men's consciences. Every objector, then, regardless of the basis for his belief, could qualify—for example, atheists as well as religious believers.

In the United States, about one out of every 350 registrants in 1966 was a conscientious objector. The proportion is rising (in the ten years from 1952-1962, it was one in 600). But the rise, says Arlo Tatum, does not seem to be related to the Vietnam war so much as to the civil rights movement, which brought a new consciousness of individual rights to many, especially Negroes; and to Pope John XXIII's Encyclical, *Pacem in Terris,* published in 1963. The Pope gave strong approval to conscientious objection, noting that "if civil authorities legislate . . . anything that is contrary to that [moral] order and therefore contrary to the will of God, neither the laws made nor the authorization granted can be binding on the conscience of the citizen since we must obey God rather than men." Prior to the Pope's words, Catholics were rarely found among conscientious objectors. Now, they represent by far the largest increase in new applicants within church groups, says Tatum.

It would seem that a democratic society could make better provisions for the protection of men's consciences, and this is surely a subject that a Congressional inquiry on the draft should explore. Our present strict policies appear to jeopardize national security and American values more than protect them. From the military point of view, it would seem that throwing boys into Vietnam who violently oppose the war could only lower morale and endanger other American boys' lives. On the home front, even General Hershey admits that "we are turning protesters into martyrs." Some are going to prison (450 draft violators were convicted in 1966), and others are fleeing to Canada, which has no conscription. Although these boys have been castigated as "draft-dodgers," we are wrong to write them off so quickly as cowards and irresponsible citizens. It is comforting to believe they are the dregs of our younger generation, but this is not true, as professors on any campus will confirm. Said Dr. Edgar Z. Friedenberg, professor of sociology at the University of California: "One fact that is often overlooked is that most of the college students who have been active in protest movements are among the better students—and those in positions of intellectual leadership on their own campuses. Certainly these are not people with a record of failure and disaffection in the system. . . . They have developed unusual moral courage." [5]

To many of these boys, who may make substantial contributions to America, we offer only the painful alternatives: prison or Canada. Fleeing to Canada means permanent exile, for the boy can never set foot in the United States again without facing criminal prosecution. In the seventeenth and eighteenth centuries, European societies persecuted our founding fathers for their beliefs. Today, we are similarly persecuting some of our own young men. Arlo Tatum helps put the situation in historical perspective by wryly observing: "I have never heard our forefathers called 'draft-dodgers,' nor have I heard the boys going to Canada called pilgrims."

In the South the draft is carrying on another type of persecution which is not traced to national policy, but which Selective Service condones by its silence. White draft officials are using the power of the draft to punish Negroes. The bizarre lengths to which all-white Selective Service systems will go is illustrated by the case of 24-year-old James Jolliff of Mississippi. Several years ago he was classified 4-F because of epilepsy. In the summer of 1966 he became president of the local chapter of the National Association for the Advancement of Colored People. Soon after, he was reclassified 1-A and ordered for induction. He protested, but a local doctor under contract to the armed forces declared him fit. The state director of Selective Service was then informed of Jolliff's epileptic condition, and promised an examination in a Veteran's Administration hospital. Instead Jolliff was returned to the same doctor who again pronounced him qualified for the Army. Jolliff was then literally whisked away at night to Fort Polk and inducted before he could contact his lawyers. Finally, his lawyers were able to get him taken to Fort Sam Houston, Brook Medical Center, where doctors confirmed he had epilepsy. He was given a medical discharge.

In another case, it is charged that the state director of the draft in Mississippi, Colonel James L. Davis, intervened to have three criminal prosecutions that were pending against civil rights worker John Sumrall dropped so that he could be drafted. In November, 1966, the Lawyers Committee for Civil Rights Under the Law brought suit in Sumrall's behalf, charging that Davis attempted to accelerate Sumrall's induction. The suit also charges that the drafting of Negroes by all-white boards is unconstitutional and asks that boards be enjoined from drafting any Negroes until Negroes are properly represented on the boards.

Civil rights lawyers in Mississippi contend there is not a single Negro board member or clerk in the entire state draft system, and that Negro civil rights workers are regularly drafted before whites of identical eligibility. Said Charles Evers, civil rights leader: "Until Negroes are appointed to these boards, the draft will continue to be used in Mississippi as a weapon to punish civil rights leaders and undermine the civil rights movement."

General Hershey has long known of and openly admitted the racially biased composition of draft boards in the South. For a man who does not shirk from exercising power, he has been unforgivably derelict in not demanding that Negroes be appointed to local boards and that the abusive discrimination against black registrants be halted.

9 ☆ The Military Accomplice

Joseph W. Namath is a twenty-three-year-old all-star rookie quarterback for the New York Jets professional football team. Upon signing his contract with the Jets he received $400,000 and a green Lincoln Continental as inducements to exhibit his physical prowess and endurance on the gridiron. Joseph W. Namath is also classified 4-F, unfit for military duty because of an injury to his right knee, which involved a torn ligament and the surgical removal of cartilage. Anticipating raised eyebrows over the physical rejection of a famous football star, the Department of Army issued an explanation to all Congressmen in December, 1965.

> It may seem illogical [said the Army] that an individual who is physically active in civilian athletics should be found unfit for military service. When playing professional football, it must be presumed that Mr. Namath does so with the counsel and preparation of doctors and trainers. He is closely watched and professional assistance is close at hand at every game and practice session. In the military service, these conditions would not necessarily be present. In Vietnam, for example, the life and

safety of his comrades could depend on Namath performing his duties under extremely adverse conditions.

After reading the bulletin a Congressman remarked to his staff: "Perhaps they could assign him to the Pentagon. There must be medics there who could treat his leg if he fell over a paper clip." The Congressman was not being simply facetious, nor was he unwise to the motives of the military. The Army, like Selective Service, is engaged in the paradoxical game of pretending to need men desperately while turning down as many as possible. General Hershey's office and the Army have, as one close student of the draft put it, "a slick routine to keep the draft going and maintain the illusion of the universality of service." Selective Service sends off a large percentage of our manpower into the netherland of arbitrary deferments. Then the Defense Department, which sets standards of acceptance, refuses to accept half of all the men who get as far as the Armed Forces Examining and Entrance Stations. Joe Namath is to the armed forces what George Hamilton is to Selective Service—the pinnacle of absurdity in the conspiracy to preserve the draft.

We can hardly expect the military to be enthusiastic about any measure that would threaten the draft. It was the military hierarchy who forced the peacetime draft upon us in 1948. Even so, they viewed it only as a consolation prize from Congress. They had bigger things in mind. Since 1918, the military establishment has persistently attempted to bring every young man under their authority by inducing Congress to endorse universal military training. Unlike our present "selective" draft, UMT would be permanent, free from periodic Congressional renewal, and would require every boy at a certain age to enter the service for from six months to a year, and then serve in the reserves for several years.

Throughout World War II, high-ranking officers carefully laid a ground-work for post-war conscription. Later, several soldiers exposed this activity. Lieutenant Colonel Roscoe Conkling, on

the Selective Service staff, charged that officers who were supposedly handling urgent matters in the daily conduct of the war
"spent most of their time" in July and August, 1944 "drafting
legislation for compulsory military training." [1] The Army spent
thousands of dollars to illegally publicize UMT. Its chief advocate, General George C. Marshall, later Secretary of State and
Secretary of Defense, was so certain of Congressional approval of
UMT that he instructed officers to procede with plans as if it
already were in effect. UMT was voted down after the war, but
the military did not lose completely. They won the peacetime
draft in 1948.

In his book, *The Military Establishment,* Dr. John M. Swomley, Jr., a long-time scholar of the draft, describes the military's
fight for conscription. He charges that officials created a phony
war scare of Russia in the spring of 1948 to obtain huge military
concessions from Congress, including the peacetime draft. "The
Army even went so far as to hand President Truman an intelligence report which 'pictured the Soviet Army as on the move'
when 'actually the Soviets were redistributing their troops to
spring stations,' " charges Swomley. The foreign press called the
crisis with Russia "Washington-inspired," as did Hanson Bald-
win, military editor of *The New York Times,* who said we had
been led to believe "there would be war before the harvest." [2]

Almost immediately after President Truman's emergency
message to Congress on March 17, 1948, asking for UMT and
Selective Service, the war scares mysteriously vanished. By May
14 of that year, *U.S. News & World Report* noted that "it was
proving more difficult to turn off than to turn on the war psychology" generated in Congress "by high officials only a few
weeks ago." In retrospect Swomley considers it difficult to
understand how so many Congressmen, tricked into reviving the
draft, were "deceived" by "the way in which the war crisis was
created." Some Congressmen, he believes, were willing to ignore
the means to justify measures they favored and "others were
swept along with the general hysteria."

The military appears to be committed to keeping the draft, and expanding it if possible, as an arm of its own power. With completely volunteer forces, in the absence of a draft, the military jurisdiction would extend perhaps over three million men at the most. Under today's Selective Service, the military has at its command some 33 million men. Not only does the draft force highly skilled men into the military at slave wages, but it affords the military a far-reaching sphere of influence over the country's economy, educational institutions and politics that would rapidly end with the demise of Selective Service. This explains why sound arguments against the draft as an inefficient mechanism to procure men often fail. Swomley insists that the real issue in the struggle to preserve the draft is "civilian versus military control of society." Even Dwight D. Eisenhower has warned us against the dangers of the ever-growing "military-industrial complex."

This chapter is entitled "The Military Accomplice" to illustrate the part the military establishment plays in helping Selective Service survive. In awful fact, the true distinction between the military powers and draft powers has been effectively erased; Selective Service is almost totally controlled by military interests. It is appalling that the roster of Selective Service, allegedly a *civilian* organization, reads like a directory of the Pentagon. Among the state directors of the draft are Colonel Fred M. Croom, (Arkansas); Brigadier General Ernest E. Novey (Connecticut); Major General John E. Walsh (Idaho); Lieutenant Colonel Everett S. Stephenson (Kentucky); Colonel Samuel F. Gray (New Mexico); Colonel Lloyd Charles Wilson (Rhode Island); Captain Charles L. Kessler, USNR (Virginia). In only four states (Alabama, Massachusetts, North Carolina and Oregon) do we have draft directors with 'Mr.' before their names. The military clique is in full power at Selective Service headquarters. Besides General Hershey, who is virtual dictator of the operation, all of the fourteen key officials but two are colonels or captains. So all-pervasive is the military influence in Selective

Service that few citizens even realize that Congress intended it to be a civilian agency. The first director of Selective Service, appointed in 1940, was a civilian, Clarence Dykstra, then president of the University of Wisconsin. After six months in the position, he retired because of ill health and was succeeded by General Hershey. Surely, an important reform that Congress should immediately consider is returning Selective Service to civilian control.

A few years ago, it was noted that the armed forces were rejecting an ever-greater percentage of young men for physical, mental and moral deficiencies. Many persons misinterpreted this to mean that our youth was "the flabby generation," and that our school system which had produced such "uneducated" boys was on a dangerous decline. The rejection rates were offered, and too often accepted, as proof that our young men were on the road to deterioration. In 1964, Congressman Curtis saw it from another perspective: "Of course, there is another way of looking at this [high] statistic on rejections. Perhaps the military criteria for physical and mental fitness . . . is simply a more convenient way for them to eliminate the numbers subject to the draft which is in excess to their needs."

Curtis' appraisal, of course, was correct. Dr. Harold Wool, director for procurement policy of the Department of Defense, finally admitted in 1966 at the University of Chicago draft conference that the higher rejection rate was caused by stiffer standards and not softer men. The mental aptitude test standards, in particular, he noted has been rising gradually.

The armed forces standards are conveniently juggled—both reset and reinterpreted by examiners—to regulate the flow of acceptable men. Like Selective Service, the Defense Department must devise ways to get rid of the enormous surplus of men available through the draft. Operating under the "philosophy of abundance," as General Hershey calls it, the military can afford to be ultra-selective. Today the armed forces have become so cavalier in their choices that one authority terms it "an insolent dissipation of manpower." Standards are far higher than the law requires. After Selective Service reduces the 1-A manpower pool to 8 per cent of the draftable males, the Pentagon comes along and chops in half the tiny piece of manpower, so carefully collected from this nation, and discards it as "unfit for military service." It almost boggles the mind to contemplate that, of those taking the preinduction or induction examination, one out of every two young American males, in short, the bulk of American vitality—who hold civilian jobs, father the nation's progeny, keep communities, companies, colleges running—is so casually dropped in the trash can by the military. In fiscal 1965, a total of 479,896 men were judged unfit for service, about 43 per cent for mental reasons, 54 per cent for physical reasons, and 2 per cent for "administrative" reasons—homosexuality, criminal tendencies or records, drug addiction and other character traits that make them unsuited "To associate with military personnel."

After World War II, while General Hershey busily expanded deferments, the Defense Department upped the standards. During World War I and World War II, when men were scarce, the combined rejection rate was 30 per cent. In the Korean War 37 per cent of the men were turned away. After the war, when peacetime produced many more men than the military could handle, rejection figures increased steadily, reaching 49 per cent in 1961. After that, military examiners were forced to refuse more men than they accepted. In 1962, they rejected 54 per cent; in 1963, 56.1 per cent, and in 1964, the year the youngsters from the post-World War II baby boom hit draft age, examiners were frantically finding ways to say no. That year the rejection rate rose to an all-time high of 57.9 per cent; nearly six out of ten boys (twice the rate during World War II) were called unfit for service on one pretext or other.

In 1965, the rejection rated dropped to 50.1, primarily because after President Johnson's call for more draftees, the Department of Defense condescended to take *high school gradu-*

ates who had otherwise failed the armed forces academic tests. When asked how many men this new policy would release into the manpower pool, General Hershey asserted "very few." He insists there is no way to obtain exact figures, for they are kept only by local boards. The secrecy of numbers in this case is convenient. An unpublished document prepared by the Defense Department showed that 52.7 per cent of all the men failing the armed forces mental aptitude test (the Armed Forces Qualifying Test) were high school graduates. Some were even college graduates. Each year then prior to the "lowered standards" (effective November, 1965) about 110,000 high school graduates sent to the Army through the draft were refused induction for academic incompetency. It is small wonder that the Hershey-Pentagon team would not want the figure publicized. Revealing the great number of educated who fail to qualify might highlight the basic contradiction permeating all Selective Service, one officials would rather leave undiscussed: Why does the Army pretend to beckon men with one hand and with the other turn thumbs down? Is it fair to ask us to suffer a draft when the Army—to preserve the system —must become so intellectually elite as to reject hundreds of thousands of men who have received the highest blessing of America's public education system?

By December, 1966, the overall rejection rate for the armed forces had dropped to 40 per cent to accommodate the need for more soldiers in Vietnam. Although this current rate is unusually low for the United States in recent years, it is still incredibly high when compared with the rejection rates for the armed forces of other countries. In 1963, a report to the subcommittee on Employment and Manpower of the Senate Committee on Labor and Public Welfare showed the rejection rates of some NATO countries: Belgium, 8 per cent; Denmark, 14 per cent; France, 18 per cent; Greece, 5 per cent; Italy, 8 per cent; Netherlands, 24 per cent; Norway, 25 per cent; Turkey, 1 per cent.[4]

A major reason for our high rejection rate is that we, unlike other nations, insist that our soldiers be perfect physical specimens, fit for combat, although only four out of five soldiers at the most ever see combat. Even during World War II, 80 per cent of the troops were in the rear echelon, performing typically civilian tasks, such as driving trucks, sorting mail, filing forms, cooking chow, dispensing supplies, handling communications and performing administrative tasks. Many famous soldiers, who apparently stood up well in combat, would be screened out by present standards. George Washington would be excluded from today's army because of decayed teeth. Teddy Roosevelt (bad eyes) and Eddie Rickenbacker (flat feet) would be 4-F. Our current physical standards are so high, and so illogical that an official at the Pentagon says they remind him of "the early days of World War II. Every draftee had to have eyeteeth that met properly. When someone bothered to find out why, we learned that this had been necessary in the days when soldiers bit the covers off packaged bullets."

Does it matter that an officer manning a missile station is overweight? that a typist has a perforated eardrum? that a radar expert has flat feet? Yet we continue to apply the outmoded concept that every soldier, no matter what his duties, be combat-perfect. Nearly all foreign countries assign conscripts to various types of jobs depending upon their physical qualifications. The Germans in World War II had ten physical categories, including those for one-eyed and one-legged men, who adequately handled office tasks. It seems unrealistic, wasteful and faintly ridiculous for the United States, with its emphasis on sophisticated weapons systems, to pursue the old-fashioned personnel policy that every military man must meet the physical requirements of an infantryman.

The mental qualifications for military service are also so high that they exclude many citizens who are gainfully employed in civilian life. Even men with fourth-grade educations are competent enough to drive taxi cabs, operate elevators, repair furniture, work in restaurants. These men, however, are not acceptable to the armed forces. A recent study by the U. S. Army Personnel Research Office shows that men declared 4-F for mental incompetency and thus prohibited by federal law from serving, on the average have a ninth-grade education. Those relegated to 1-Y because of educational deficiencies have on the average completed ten and a half years of school.[5] During World War II, men were accepted if their mental capabilities reflected a fourth-grade educational level. Under World War II standards, the countless 1-Y's now rejected for mental deficiencies would have been inducted without a second look.

The suspicious mind may also find of interest the fact that the mental qualifications of the armed forces are so constructed as to automatically increase the number of rejectees as the draftable population increases. Each potential soldier is given the Armed Forces Qualifying Test (AFQT). His passing does not depend on raw score, but on percentile, in other words, how he measures up with other men who take the test. If a man scores below the 10th percentile he is 4-F, automatically excluded from induction. If he scores from the 10th through 30th percentile, he becomes a 1-Y on mental grounds unless he is a high-school graduate; then he must score in only the 16th percentile to be drafted. With this built-in rejection scale, the armed forces must always reject from one to three out of every ten men, even though they are better equipped mentally than soldiers of other years. In a nation of geniuses, our existing draft policies would still turn away 10 to 30 per cent as mentally unqualified.

The Army has a recruiting poster: "Join the New Action Army," and above in smaller print: "If you're good enough." There are some doubts that the Army does want all the enlistees it can get, even if they are good enough. An overflow of volunteers might make the draft unnecessary. It is charged that the armed forces deliberately refuses to accept more than a certain quota of enlistees. Republican Congressmen studying the draft in 1964 insisted: "One source within the executive branch claims that the services are forbidden to accept voluntary enlistments beyond a point which the military feels would threaten the draft law. Unfortunately, there is probably no way to prove or document this assertion."

Congressman Curtis, however, is certain it is true. He says: "It has been candidly admitted by Army recruiting sergeants in private conversation that beyond a certain point they are quietly advised 'from above' . . . not to recruit any more young men . . . because if Army recruiting figures showed how easy it is for the Army to meet its force level through voluntary enlistments, Congress would review the necessity of the draft." [6] Curtis stood up on the floor of the House and challenged the armed forces to prove or disprove his charge by allowing a number of recruiting sergeants to be put under oath to testify about this practice. The only response from the Pentagon was silence.

Evidence that the Army curtails enlistments is not new. Swomley in *The Military Establishment* cites numerous instances of deceitful practices to keep enlistments down. After World War II, for example, the military fought hard for and won an extension of the draft act in 1946 on the pretense that the armed forces could not attract enough volunteers. In truth the Army was forced to desperate measures to support this claim, reports Swomley. The law forbade the issuance of draft calls if the enlistments during the previous three months were adequate to support the Army's authorized number of men. In order to legally issue draft calls for September and October, 1946, the Army first had to prematurely discharge some 300,000 men six months before their enlistment term expired. Then, of course, it insisted it needed draftees as replacements.

In 1948, Representative Paul Shafer of Michigan told the House that he knew of one recruiting officer who was allowed only twelve recruits in a month, which he easily obtained in a week. Shafer also charged that the Army set a quota on Puerto Ricans and Negroes, accepting only enough to make up 10 per cent of the total Army strength.

Another suspicious coincidence occurred in 1949, when it

seemed certain that recruitments would meet President Truman's armed forces quota for June 30, 1950 (when the draft law expired). Prior to the renewal date, the Army made several moves to thwart enlistments. It ended two-year enlistments, accepting men for three years only; it raised mental qualifications for enlistees; and sliced two million dollars off its advertising budget for recruiting for the coming year.[7]

The Army has another peculiar practice that seems fashioned to keep enlistments down. The academic standards for enlistees are *higher* than those for draftees. A high school graduate who is drafted must score in only the 16th percentile on the armed forces qualifying test; but in order to enlist, this same man has to score in the 21st percentile or above. A non-high school graduate can be *drafted* if he achieves the 21st percentile or above, but the Army will not accept the same high-school dropout for *enlistment* unless he scores in the 31st percentile, which is substantially higher. As Gaylord Nelson pointed out: "So we have a situation in which we are drafting into the Army men who achieve a percentile of 21 and who do not want to be in the Army and rejecting men who receive a percentile of 28, 29 or 30 on the grounds that that is not high enough for a volunteer." The Army (which requires a higher score on the AFQT than other services) in fiscal 1964 turned away 70,000 men who wished to volunteer but could not qualify under the high standards. Nelson noted in 1964 that during the previous three years 91,000 men came in through the draft who would have been refused had they volunteered.[8]

Recruiting stations administer a mental pre-screening test, the EST (Enlistment Screening Test) to prospective enlistees. If the sergeant feels a man did well enough, he can send him to the armed forces examining center to take the official qualifying test (AFQT). The recruiting officer can also refuse to forward the man for testing. That only 1 per cent of all prospective enlistees sent through recruiting channels *fail* the AFQT attests to the tough screening by recruiters. It is not unreasonable to speculate

that the pre-screening enlistment tests could be effectively misused to screen out not only the legitimately unqualified, but also
the unwanted excess.

In August, 1966, the Pentagon announced a radical new in-
cursion of the military and the draft into civilian life. The Defense Department stated its intention to draft disadvantaged
young men, about thirty per cent of them Negroes, and rehabilitate them as part of the war on poverty. In a speech before the
Veterans of Foreign Wars, Secretary of Defense McNamara forecast that the armed forces would take 40,000 men before June
30, 1967, and 100,000 each year following, who otherwise
could not qualify for service (they scored from the 10th to the
31st percentile on the AFQT) primarily because of educational
deficiencies. McNamara tied the armed forces program to the Administration's anti-poverty program: "Some of those citizens [to
be taken in] such an Army will be men emerging from another
battle: the battle of built-in poverty." He further referred to the
Department of Defense as "the largest single educational complex that the world has ever possessed."

Representative Schwengel, commenting on the prospect of using the military to solve social problems, said in 1964: "There
are those who, determined to continue the draft, advocate utilization of the draft to solve other serious national problems—utterly divorced from real or emergency military needs. This concept is . . . dangerous, for it . . . would move us further in
the direction of a highly centralized state under increased military control. President Johnson's war on poverty might mean the
uplifting of our underprivileged citizens—or it could mean a
thoroughly regimented social order."

The questions should be asked: Is such a nonmilitary function within the rightful province of a military organization? Do
we want to turn over to the military the responsibility for solving
our social and educational problems—even a portion of them?
Many Congressmen think not, as demonstrated by their action
in 1965 when they refused funds for a Pentagon plan called

STEP to accept and rehabilitate *volunteers;* the legislators deemed social rehabilitation an improper function of the armed forces. Without special funds, McNamara is now implementing a program similar to STEP, and including not only volunteers but draftees, apparently against Congesssional wishes. Congress at least should explore the issue fully. Any Congressional inquiry into the draft should surely question the propriety of McNamara's "Salvation Army."

An especially regrettable aspect of the McNamara program is that it forces the Air Force, the Marines and the Navy to accept a certain percentage of the disadvantaged—both draftees and volunteers—although these services, because of excellent recruiting programs, have been remarkably free of dependence on the draft. To absorb the 100,000 youth yearly, the Army is required to accept 25 per cent of its quarterly quotas from the disadvantaged group; the Marines 18 per cent, and the Navy and Air Force 15 per cent. To do so, the Navy, Air Force and Marines will undoubtedly be forced to refuse volunteers with higher mental qualifications. It seems inevitable that a coerced reliance on the draft, never before necessary to any degree, will damage the recruiting programs which these services so carefully built up and regard with pride. It seems almost cruel and unusual punishment. And, of course, ultimately we shall all suffer, for any further entrenchment of the draft is detrimental to us all.

10 ☆ Proposals for Reform

Without the Vietnam war, the draft might have continued to exist, virtually unnoticed, further insinuating itself into American life. Perhaps never before in this century has the draft engendered such a sense of frustration and bitter resentment in the American people. We must now take care not to let this national feeling of outrage be dissipated without effect, drained of its power to gain significant reforms, for we do not know when such opportunity for an intensive look at the draft may pass this way again. It is important that we not be deceived by token reforms offered by an administration eager to quiet criticism of the war and the draft, or coerced by expediency into an acceptance of and commitment to the draft because of the war. It is a political reality that in reforming the draft we must consider the ongoing war; but we must also think beyond it.

Unfortunately, the draft debate has been mired in superficialities. We have been sidetracked into endless discussions of the merits and drawbacks of proposals for minor changes designed to make the draft more palatable. The Administration, pro-draft Congressmen and General Hershey deliberately encourage this diversionary pastime, for it keeps our minds off the crucial issue: the deep-down corruption of the draft and whether it is necessary or desirable at all.

The numerous evils of the draft, both major and minor, which are discussed in this book, should be remedied simply because they are insulting to our intelligence and concepts of justice. These would be "nice" reforms. But most emphatically, plastic surgery will not transform the ugly Selective Service System into a thing of beauty. Prettying up the draft will make it more acceptable, but no less basically offensive. As Professor Kenneth Boulding said: "Those of us who are realistically concerned about the survival of our country should probably not waste too much time complaining about the inequities and absurdities of the draft or attempt the hopeless task of rectifying it when the plain fact is that the draft can only begin to approach 'justice' in time of major war, and a peacetime draft has to be absurd and unjust by its very nature. The axe should be applied to the root of the tree, not to its branches, and a little bug spray on the branches will not allay the rottenness of the trunk." [1]

Unquestionably, in my opinion, the only solution to our draft problems which is in keeping with American values is to abolish the draft and to replace it with a volunteer army—which, as we shall see, is feasible. But, as Senator Maurine Neuberger of Oregon told participants at the University of Chicago draft conference: "We must face the political realities." The political realities to Senator Neuberger and the three other Congressmen who were present came down to this: It is almost unthinkable that Congress would sanction, or that President Johnson would allow, the end of the draft as long as we are involved in a sizeable Vietnam war.

This does not mean that we should lessen to any degree our insistence on abolishing the peacetime draft or shrink from setting in motion the machinery which will achieve that goal. But the unpredictability of the Vietnam war, with its political implications for the draft, does mean we can expect a longer transitional period for phasing out the draft than might otherwise be necessary.

In the interim, in the words of Emerson, "If you can't be free, be as free as you can." We should by June 30, 1967, attempt to get immediate draft reforms which will end the most flagrant abuses of the draft, mainly the unfairness of illogical deferments; its use as a coercive instrument of social planning (General Hershey's "channeling"); the suppression of individual rights, and the creation of nonexistent manpower crises to spread anxiety and fear. As noted previously, we must also insist on a thorough Congressional investigation of Selective Service before we can know all the existing evils we must fight.

Although the draft needs sweeping reform, many draft reformers are notably timid in their proposals. They limit their reforms to correction of a number of petty abuses. They propose only such measures as installing computers in Selective Service, limiting the age of board members, setting national standards for deferment, making word changes in Selective Service forms. Such remedies, though needed, are not adequate. Some reformers who are bolder would saddle us with such misguided schemes as universal military service (UMT) and "national service"—which would give us relief from draft inequities, but would create far greater evils.

The single large-scale plan of merit, it seems to me (besides the eventual abolition of the draft) is the lottery proposed by Senator Edward Kennedy. The Senator's plan offers a very sensible, easily adoptable, stop-gap measure for erasing present evils until we can do away with the draft entirely. When only a few men are needed from the large manpower supply, and most deferments are meaningless, as today, a lottery seems much more fair than the arbitrary decisions made by 4,000 draft boards with no national standards.

Essentially, Kennedy would draft men by lottery at age nineteen out of a national pool. He envisions it as working this way: All men reaching age eighteen would be examined, and those physically and mentally qualified for service would be assigned a number by the local boards. After numbers are assigned, Selective Service would conduct a national drawing once a year. "It would put into a 'fishbowl,' " says Kennedy, "as many numbers as the largest local draft board in the country has registrants; then draw out each number and make a record of the order in which it appeared. Each local board would receive a copy of this list. The men whose numbers were selected first, and were therefore higher on the list, would be called first, and so on down the line. Let's assume the first number chosen in the drawing was 508. Every eligible draftee in every local board who held number 508 would know he would be called up first in the next draft call. Every eligible draftee with a number near the bottom of the list would know he would not be drafted, except in event of national emergency.

"Each number would, of course, represent a different quota of men: 508 would be held by fewer men than 35 because fewer local boards have 508 men. Before issuing a [monthly] draft call, the Selective Service System would decide how many men it needed, then compute how many numbers would have to be called to supply that many men." [2] Although Selective Service would compute its needs monthly, as dictated by Pentagon manpower requests, this does not mean that that there would be a *monthly* lottery, and that a boy would be thrown into renewed uncertainty every month, as many are now. The drawing would be held only *once a year,* to provide Selective Service with a list showing the order of call-up. From then on, Selective Service would just go down the list each month, checking off as many numbers as needed to supply the required quota of soldiers. It's hardly likely (short of grave emergency) that the list would be exhausted in a year. For example, in 1967, 1.8. million boys will turn nineteen, and an estimated 600,000 will be needed to keep forces at the current level. It is probable that Selective Service would need to go down through little more than half of a lottery list to obtain these men. (Forty per cent of the 1.8 million will be disqualified by present rejection rates).

A boy whose number is not reached during the year of his draw would be virtually invulnerable to the draft. His number would go to the bottom of the next year's list as a precaution against a national emergency. But he would not be called unless world conditions worsened drastically, so that our annual pool of eighteen- and nineteen-year-olds was not large enough to fill draft requirements.

Inducting boys at an earlier age, instead of waiting until their lives are more settled, would please both the public and the military. The Pentagon has long urged drafting younger men because they make better soldiers. At the June House hearings, the Defense Department once again recommended reversing the present age priorities from "older first" to "younger first," making nineteen-year-olds subject to the first calls. When a 1964 Gallup poll asked Americans at what age they would rather have a son enter military service, they overwhelmingly said they favored earlier service: 54 per cent replied at "eighteen or earlier," and 20 per cent said "nineteen to twenty." Only 26 per cent favored the "twenty-one or older" policy which now exists.

Kennedy's lottery would allow no deferments for marriage, fatherhood, dependency or occupations—only for extreme hardship. Students would be granted deferments for four years only (Kennedy would defer no one for graduate school). After finishing college, the boy would then take his chances in that year's lottery of nineteen-year-olds. As Kennedy contends: "Everyone—rich and poor, college and noncollege, married and single—would take his chances on an even footing."

Hershey's clipped comment on the lottery is: "I have no use for it." Hershey insists a lottery "substitutes chance for judgment." He says: "People on local boards have more compassion than a machine. The machine cannot tell whether a man is more valuable as a father or student or scientist or doctor than as a soldier." Nevertheless, the chance judgments of a lottery could hardly be as objectionable as the human ones that now prevail. As Geoffrey Hazard, professor of law at the University of Chicago, noted: "The present system is random in an unrandom sense; it has the unpredictability and irrationality of a lottery without its decency."

Bill Mauldin said: "Let's admit it, the draft is a giant crap game," as indeed it is. Whether a boy is drafted depends on his education, intelligence, socio-economic status, his pull, his profession, even the state and street where he lives, and most of all, on the unpredictable personalities of those powerful citizens who people his draft board. Kennedy's lottery would end such unfairness. It would also eliminate other worse draft evils: a boy's years of uncertainty in which he is not able to get a job or plan his future; General Hershey's abominable channeling, and student exemptions. Although Kennedy advocates student deferments, to give the armed forces trained and skilled men, students eventually would have no greater chance of escaping from the draft than boys from lower educational and socio-economic levels. We can expect, however, that boys, being human, would enter college to put off for four years the possibility of going to Vietnam, hoping the war would be over by then. Continuing blanket deferment of college students will not end charges of class privilege or illegal group deferments. But Kennedy's plan is preferable to the present one in which proportionately fewer college students ever serve at all. Ultimately, Kennedy's plan would probably result in disproportionately greater numbers of college men serving because they, unlike 20 per cent of their less well-educated countrymen, are almost certain to pass the armed forces mental qualifying test.

So illogical are General Hershey's stated objections to the lottery that it makes one suspect they are not the real ones. Hershey complains that a lottery would not allow rapid expansion of the armed forces in a crisis. Actually, flexibility is one of the greatest assets of a lottery: As many or as few men could be called up as desired to meet widely fluctuating manpower needs. No one has suggested, as Hershey implies, making the nineteen-year-olds who are not called immediately forever exempt. A man will have the assurance, if his number is not high on the list, that he will be temporarily exempt under present conditions. But he will be liable up to age twenty-six in case a national emergency demands large numbers of men quickly.

Another straw man Hershey sets up is that the lottery would provide no physical or mental standards, no exemptions or deferments. His favorite illustration for discrediting the lottery is: "In the Armed Forces, I can see them, by the time we drew a one-legged man as No. 1 and say 'Here is your first boy,' you immediately know what would happen." This rhetoric is tomfoolery and the General knows it. All men would be examined as usual and found qualified *before* their numbers were put into a lottery. Nor would legitimate hardship deferments be denied. But we would no longer have outrageous hardship deferments, like the one given to actor George Hamilton. In a lottery, the millions of senseless deferments, now granted merely to soak up the manpower excess, would be eliminated.

It is probable that the country would react favorably to a lottery. It is used today in Australia, West Germany, and several other countries, with reported success. In the Civil War, both the North and the South used lotteries, but they were administered on a local level, and the people believed them to be corrupt. When a national lottery was used in World War I, and three times at the beginning of World War II, even General Hershey admits there were no charges of dishonesty: "I don't think they accused us of being crooked." The lottery was dropped in March of 1942 because, by that time, most boys were being taken as soon as they reached draft age, making the lottery an unnecessary waste of time.

Today Hershey argues that the public will not accept the lottery because it is accustomed to Selective Service. "Despite the criticism of deferments which are alleged to favor this group or that," he says, "the people of the United States generally believe that selection for military service must be accompanied by judgment, and not rest solely upon the chance of a draw." [3]

Anthropologist Margaret Mead, on the other hand, believes Americans are more apt to accept a mechanical lottery than the present system. She says: "The less the lottery system contains elements which are seen as subject to manipulation, the less resentment there is. Ideally, therefore, what is needed is a draft system in which the lottery system works with impeccable impersonality. . . . The more impersonal the lottery, the fewer the exemptions and exceptions, in fact the fewer human decisions involved, the less there will be a feeling that decisions are fixed [rigged] and arbitrary, and the greater the acceptance of the chance results will be." [4]

Two other drastic proposals for draft reform must be mentioned briefly because in 1966 they received wide publicity, and some persons still proselytize for them. Fortunately, both proposals now appear to be dying deserving deaths. In the September, 1966, *Reader's Digest,* Dwight D. Eisenhower capitalized on the current debate over draft inequities to try to stimulate revival of a military dream, also dear to such old-timers as General Hershey and L. Mendel Rivers, chairman of the House Armed Services Committee. These men favor drafting *every* young man under a plan known as universal military training (UMT).

The senior citizens of the military have pushed UMT for many a year now, most fervently since World War II. Congress has repeatedly voted it down. In 1951, there was a flurry of support for UMT, when it was feared the nation was in danger of imminent nuclear attack, and that a disciplined cadre of all the nation's young men would be vital to civil defense, especially in restoring order after an atomic attack. In 1951, Congress approved UMT in principle—hence our misnamed draft act of today, the Universal Military Training and Service Act of 1951. But by 1952, Congress was unwilling to go through with it. The

House killed UMT by refusing to approve specific plans for its implementation. General Hershey was so outraged that he suggested they could use the existing draft law to override Congressional intent and draft everyone anyway, in effect, creating UMT. His suggestion was met with utter silence.

Eisenhower, in his recent plea, made little case for UMT as militarily advantageous, except to note that "After a few years of UMT, we would have always a huge reserve of young men with sound basic military training." True! Except that the last thing the Pentagon and most military advisors want today is a mammoth corps of half-trained reservists, whose training and upkeep would be tremendously costly and add nothing to military effectiveness. At a time when the military is attempting to build a small, highly trained force of men to use today's sophisticated weapons, UMT would be a grave liability. Hershey admits the Pentagon throws up its hands in horror at UMT. Suggesting it to the military, he says, makes him "as popular as a bastard at a family reunion."

Eisenhower argued that UMT would end draft inequalities, and indeed it would, but only by virtue of this misguided logic: "If we can't decide how to draft the few we need, let's draft them all." At the core of Ike's devotion to UMT is the conviction—shared by all UMT advocates—that a stint in the military molds a man's character and benefits society. One wonders why military men in particular seem obsessed with this mission to better the citizenry through military experience. But scratch a UMT proponent, and that is what you invariably find.

As the former President put it: "Although I certainly do not contend that UMT would be a cure for juvenile deliquency, I do think it could do much to stem the growing tide of irresponsible behavior and outright crime in the United States. To expose all our young men for a year to discipline and *the correct attitudes of living* [emphasis added] inevitably would straighten out a lot of potential troublemakers. In this connection—although I am sure that in saying this I label myself as old-fashioned—I deplore the beatnik dress, the long unkempt hair, the dirty necks and fingernails now affected by a minority of our boys. If UMT accomplished nothing more than to produce cleanliness and decent grooming, it might be worth the price tag—and I am not altogether jesting when I say this." [5] The price tag for inducing men to clean their fingernails and comb their hair, incidentally, is estimated at an additional $3 to $6 billion a year. For what it would cost to operate UMT, we could abolish the draft altogether and support a voluntary army, as we shall see.

Despite the prominence of persons pushing UMT, it has little appeal today. In this time of crisis over the draft, UMT stirs hardly a whisper of discussion among most draft reformers. The University of Chicago conferees, for example, found the topic so boring that after listening to a single scheduled speech, they dismissed the subject with the barest discussion.

The second draft reform proposal that caused a flurry of interest in 1966, but now generates little enthusiasm, is national service (also called "national servitude"). It is akin to UMT in that every young man—and perhaps every young woman—would be drafted for two or three years. Some would serve in the military, but the others would be assigned to a kind of domestic Peace Corps; they would spend their tour of duty working in social projects—some already in existence (those under the auspices of church groups and voluntary assistance associations)—and some to be created especially for the national service program. For example, University of Chicago sociology professor Morris Janowitz suggests a Police Cadet Corps to soak up 100,000 young men to increase the quality of our police departments; a National Teachers Corps of 150,000 young teachers or teacher's aides to improve our public school systems; an expanded National Job Corps, like the old Civilian Conservation Corps (CCC) to give opportunities to our disadvantaged youth.

National service plans vary considerably, and it must also be pointed out that some persons, including Harris Wofford, associate director of the Peace Corps, favor a *voluntary* national service, which is *decidedly* different from universal compulsory service. A voluntary national service plan would not draft everyone, but would provide a *nonmilitary option* for young men who might ordinarily be drafted. A man's service in the Peace Corps, for example, would qualify as a nonmilitary option. Some proponents, however, do not suggest that the man who serves alternative civilian duty be completely exempt from military duty, but that he be put at the bottom of the draft priorities. His civilian service in nonmilitary activities, presumably to be specified by the government, would be a kind of credit to be honored by draft officials. Although nonmilitary alternatives should be expanded to accommodate boys who can not conscientiously fight, it seems doubtful that a large-scale alternative service plan for all boys could be worked out satisfactorily—without resulting in new, widespread inequities.

Most of the plans for national service, however, are compulsory and universal. Proponents generally agree that upon registering for national service a young man—Margaret Mead would also include women—would specify his preference for military or nonmilitary service. Miss Mead, however, cautions against letting women choose military service. Drawing her conclusion from ancient societies and experiments with agression in animals, Miss Mead warns that the female, unlike the male, will fight to the finish—to the ultimate destruction of the race; whereas, "Men have nice little rules about war—like not fighting on Christmas." Ancient societies that gave women arms did not survive, contends Miss Mead, and she advises against it.

At first blush, national service seems appealing. The press and many liberals gave it an enthusiastic reception because the plan seems to offer a constructive alternative to men who don't want to fight, and at the same time provides educational and socially uplifting experiences to millions of young people. The national service proposal was sent up as a trial balloon by Secretary of Defense McNamara on May 18, 1966, in a speech before a group of newspaper editors in Montreal. At the tail end of a speech on foreign affairs, McNamara incidentally acknowledged draft inequities and uttered the following sentences that grabbed the headlines: "It seems to me that we could move toward remedying that [draft] inequity by asking every young person in the U.S. to give two years of service to his country—whether in one of the military services, in the Peace Corps or in some other volunteer developmental work at home and abroad." McNamara did not clarify what he meant by "asking," whether he was suggesting *voluntary* or *compulsory* universal service. Nearly everyone interpreted it as compulsory.

With astonishing alacrity, the nation's liberals rallied around the universal national service concept, recalling that it was not new, but had been suggested sixty years ago by the philosopher William James in *The Moral Equivalent of War.* James Reston, columnist for *The New York Times,* praised McNamara for "reaching beyond the draft, beyond the Pentagon, beyond Administration policy, beyond the present, and certainly beyond Vietnam and the present inequities of Selective Service." *The New York Times* endorsed universal national service editorially. Senator Jacob K. Javits of New York rushed to introduce legislation for working out a plan of compulsory national service. And Margeret Mead came up with the most comprehensive plan of all, as outlined in an article in *Redbook,* September, 1966, titled: "The Case for Drafting All Boys—And Girls." "No one would be exempt in the old sense," says Miss Mead. "No one would be relieved of the obligation to give two years, let us say, to the country, working under direction and living on the same subsistence allowance as everyone else."

Universal national service's moment of glory was short lived. Although some still fervently support it, serious consideration of national service as a draft reform is waning. Harvard's President Nathan Pusey was the first strong voice to speak out against the program. In his baccalaureate address in June, 1966, he labeled national service "coercive conformity," and "a colossal waste of time." He declared he could think of nothing "worse for

young people eager to get on in the world than to stand by mark-
ing time."

Most participants in the University of Chicago draft conference arrived feeling the agenda was rigged to favor universal
national service: A chief force behind the conference was Professor Janowitz, a devotee of universal national service, and it
was readily apparent that a disproportionate number of the
papers submitted were on national service. There was an aura of
expectation that national service would emerge as The Grand
Design for Draft Reform, endorsed by the nation's leading liberals and scholars. Such hopes, held by the proponents of national
service, vanished the first day, as it dawned on many conferees
what compulsory national service was all about—universal conscription of young people for nonmilitary needs. It was especially alarming to many conferees to note the active crusading
by "intellectuals" for more compulsion and expanded control of
the state over young people's lives.

Said William R. Keast, President of Wayne State University:
"It grieves me to see the readiness of people here to accept bureaucratic interference in human lives." Professor Gibson Winter,
of the University of Chicago's Divinity School, commented on
the "enthusiasm for compulsion," and Professor Richard Flacks
was distressed to see that "liberals, including Dr. Mead, seem
to have given up the idea there is something intrinsically wrong
with compulsion." It was not only disconcerting, but incredible,
to many libertarians to find themselves in the position of patiently
having to explain why in a free country it is an infringement of
personal liberty to draft our entire population of eighteen-year-
olds into a forced labor camp managed by the state, and high-
mindedly call it "national service."

National service—the universal drafting of all youth for nonmilitary purposes—is, on reflection, an outrage against a free society, and even a few years ago would have been instantly denounced as a totalitarian idea, reminiscent of Hitler's youth
corps. It is understandable that persons, such as Miss Mead,

who have found fulfillment in serving others, would want to give this opportunity to all youth; but the fact to be heavily considered in a democracy is that all youth may not want it. Nor should we think that service to the nation is restricted to organized federal and state social welfare programs. Undeniably, many young people serve their country well in the Peace Corps and other government projects. But others are contributing to the welfare of the country by working in hospitals, schools, businesses and various endeavors within the free enterprise system. It would be criminal to force our independent young people into a highly regimented federal scheme of social service. Possibly, it would also be unconstitutional. The program might well collapse at the first Supreme Court test by some fellow who objected to the draft law being misused for purposes quite unrelated to the "common defense." National service might also be declared a violation of the Thirteenth Amendment, which prohibits involuntary servitude.

In addition to its objectionable philosophy, national service gives rise to a multitude of serious problems, as even its proponents readily admit. Who could decide what social programs and organizations should be approved? If working for the American Friends Service Committee is acceptable, why not for the Black Muslims? And if the National Association for the Advancement of Colored People, why not the Student Non-Violent Coordinating Committee? Would the compulsory-voluntary service destroy such programs as the Peace Corps and Vista, successful mainly because of the great enthusiasm of their volunteers? Could we possibly create enough meaningful jobs for the 1.2 million men and 4 million women who would be thrown into the nonmilitary niches of national service every two years? How would we meet the cost—which would be staggering, considering the average cost for training one Peace Corps worker is $7,800? And would the program damage the economy by keeping 5 million young people unemployed—about 7 per cent of the entire labor force?

Finally, national service as a cure for our draft ailments

would be as effective as taking heart medicine to combat cancer. National service is totally irrelevant to our draft troubles and, as has been admitted by many, including Miss Mead, is hooked onto discussions about the draft simply to gain attention for a national program of social service that many feel is desirable on its own merits, regardless of draft injustices.

It is true that universal national service, like UMT, would end the suffering of the few by inflicting it universally. But UMT would end inequities of the draft; national service would compound them. With national service, military needs would still have to be met; the same number of men as always would have to go to fill armed forces quotas. When pressed at the University of Chicago conference on what would happen if not enough men volunteered for the armed forces under national service, Terrence Cullinan, of the Stanford Research Institute, and a crusader for the plan, retorted: "Well, of course we would have to draft them out of the nonmilitary group."

So, national service, after taking us on a wild goose chase, brings us back to the same old draft, its inequities unresolved. Senator Edward Kennedy put it precisely: "At present their program [national service] appears essentially to be the draft—with nearly all its faults—writ larger."

11 ☆ The Case for Abolishing the Draft

It is an open and, to me, shut case. Abolishing the draft is the
ultimate solution to our peacetime military needs. When I first
started writing this book, I could not be so confident, for there
was one significant obstacle that could not be discounted: a
study done by the Pentagon, which was never released, but was
widely publicized. According to Pentagon spokesmen, the study
showed a professional, all-voluntary army to be economically
unthinkable. The study, said the Pentagon, placed the additional
cost of a voluntary army as high as $17 billion. Such a cost
probably would be prohibitive, although a few Congressmen,
even after hearing the Pentagon's exorbitant cost figures,
deemed ridding ourselves of the draft would be worth it. Other
Congressmen felt the estimates were suspiciously high—but
without access to the complete study, no one could be sure.
There was a reasonable doubt about the validity of the figures.

There is no longer any doubt. I have read the suppressed Pentagon study and the figures do not show a voluntary force to be
prohibitively costly. On the contrary, the Pentagon report fore-
sees the all-voluntary army as completely feasible. There is no

real $17 billion cost barrier to abolishing the draft, as we shall see. This figure is the reddest of red herrings, thrown to the Congress and the American people to stifle an investigation into ending the draft. By raising the pay of our soldiers to a living wage, we can be well on the way to ending the draft with the end of the Vietnam crisis.

To many the prospect of recruiting a sizeable army without the draft seems strange, even startling. Abolishing the draft, at first, appears to be a radical proposal—akin to abolishing the postal service or the police force. When first confronted with the idea, most persons respond with initial disbelief or tentative smiles. Invariably, their retort to the suggestion of an all volunteer army is: "But *who* would volunteer?" Such a reaction is merely a reflection of the fact that to those of us who grew up during World War II, the draft has always existed; its existence has become self-justifying, its threat-power unquestioned. As General Hershey says: "Almost continuously for twenty-six years, i.e., since 1940, they [the American people] have accepted Selective Service as part of their way of life."

The draft is not a legitimate institution in a peacetime democracy; it need not be and should not be a constant specter in our future. Abolishing the draft is actually hardly a radical idea: It is a conservative position, rooted in the most basic American principle of freedom, and should be a goal of all those committed to the preservation of individual rights.

Abolishing the draft is politically nonpartisan. It is not associated with the "left" or the "right." It has been advocated by politicians at such opposite poles as Barry Goldwater and Adlai Stevenson. Both suggested ending the draft in their presidential campaigns, Goldwater in 1964 and Stevenson in 1956. Unfortunately, both times the proposal was discredited. The suggestion proved so embarrassing to Stevenson, running against General Eisenhower, that his advisors persuaded him to drop it from his speeches. Johnson shrugged off Goldwater's proposal as another sure sign of the idiocy of a man who favored bombing

North Vietnam. Since the inception of the peacetime draft in 1948, its abolition has never been seriously debated in public. Washington secrecy and Presidential commissions have effectively stymied free and open discussion of the subject. It is small wonder that the American people in general have thought little about the issues, problems and possibilities involved in discontinuing the draft.

First, it should be said that banishing Selective Service without revamping military personnel policies to induce men to enlist would undoubtedly leave us with a deficient number of soldiers. Coincident with plans to end the draft we must formulate incentives to make the army an attractive career: We must stop using the draft as a crutch for the armed forces, and actively build a volunteer army. Such a volunteer army presents three major considerations: cost (how much must we pay to induce men to sign up?); implications for society (will a professional army be a threat to the established social order?); the capabilities of the volunteer army in meeting fluctuating manpower requirements.

"If the Army was still using mules, we would know they were stark raving mad," said one observer of the draft, "but their treatment of men, no less nineteenth century, goes unnoticed." It is true that the military, because of its surfeit of cheap manpower supplied by the draft, flagrantly misuses its men. Pay is at subsistence level; the housing on base is deplorable; skilled men are wasted in menial jobs; soldiers perform duties that could be better done by hired civilians. Secretary McNamara recently hired 60,000 civilians to fill 75,000 jobs formerly held by soldiers.

"The draft," says Harvard's Professor John Kenneth Galbraith, "survives principally as a device by which we use compulsion to get young men to serve at less than the market rate of pay. We shift the cost of military service from the well-to-do taxpayer, who benefits by lower taxes, to the impecunious young draftee. This is a highly regressive arrangement which we would not tolerate in any other area."

Surely, our military pay must be one of the silent shames of the nation. We pay our beginning soldiers less than any other NATO country, including France and West Germany, which also depend on a draft. The pay of a private E-1 is $90 a month —little more than the pay of a Rumanian peasant on a collective farm. In 1965, Senator Gaylord Nelson told Congress that the war on poverty was being lost in, of all places, the armed forces. Some 840,000 servicemen—more than 25 per cent of the total armed forces personnel—were under the poverty line established by the federal government. According to an Air Force Report of 1964, some 71,000 Air Force men were moonlighting to make extra money, some to support families. More astounding, 5,000 Air Force personnel were on relief.[1]

Is it any wonder the military bemoans its inability to attract men without the draft? Nevertheless, the draft is self-defeating for the military; by supplying the armed forces with limitless numbers of bodies, the draft discourages the development of sound personnel policies, including higher pay, that would free the military from the draft.

No business, for example, would long survive with the turnover of personnel endured by our armed forces. Turnover produced by the draft is an increasingly critical problem, from the point of view of cost and national security. In 1957, under Eisenhower, a blue-ribbon committee headed by Ralph J. Cordiner, the President of General Electric, made a study of military efficiency. The report stated: "It is foolish for the Armed Services to obtain highly advanced weapons systems and not have men of sufficient competence to understand, operate, and maintain such equipment. . . . The solution here, of course, is not to draft more men to stand and look helplessly at the machinery. The solution is to give the men already in the armed forces the incentives required to make them want to stay in the service long enough and try hard enough to take these higher responsibilities, gain the skill and experience levels we need and then remain to give the services the full benefit of their skills." Draftees are nearly useless, said the report, for they can hardly learn the fundamentals of complicated weapons in two years.[2]

And, as the statistics show, draftees rarely serve longer than two years. From 95 to 97 per cent (estimates vary from year to year) of our conscripts can't wait to leave the service. In 1964, only 2.8 per cent of the draftees re-enlisted. Only 25 per cent of the first-term volunteers (many of whom Hershey has frightened into enlisting) sign up again—for a turnover rate of 75 per cent. Comparatively, Army career men, of the type who would make up a voluntary force, have an 85 per cent re-enlistment rate—only a 15 per cent turnover loss. Considering that the training cost of one draftee is $6,000, and that we inducted 340,000 men in fiscal 1966, by 1968 the wasted investment in these draftees alone will be an astronomical $2 billion. Cutting turnover not only makes a voluntary army more effective militarily, but offsets much of the additional payroll cost necessary to attract sufficient numbers of volunteers.

What would the cost of a voluntary army be? The truth about cost estimates is found in the secret Pentagon study. On April 18, 1964, after getting wind of a Republican drive in the House to abolish the draft, President Johnson hastily called a press conference and announced he had asked the Pentagon to do "the most complete study of the draft ever made." The alleged purpose was to determine whether the draft could be ended in this decade. Completion of the study, budgeted at $1 million, was scheduled for April, 1965.

April came and went and the study was not released, although it was an open secret that the project had been finished in March, 1965. What was once a political maneuver to steal the Republican's thunder was now a political liability. The spring of 1965 was hardly the time to talk of ending the draft—not when the President and the Joint Chiefs of Staff were preparing for a massive troop buildup in Vietnam. The Pentagon quietly shelved the draft report.

With mounting criticism of the draft, demands from Congressmen and the press to see the long-overdue study grew more insistent. Finally, in February, 1966, Harold Wool, director of procurement policy for the Defense Department and the man in charge of the study, admitted: "The study was largely completed by last summer, but the Vietnam outlook changed it, and now the basic study must be revised." [3] (In other words, the facts had to be juggled to provide a more politically acceptable conclusion.)

Four months later, at the House Armed Services hearings in June, the Pentagon pretended to stage a grand unveiling of the study; actually, they palmed off on us what amounted to a publicity release about the study's results. (The entire study has never been released, and a source close to the Pentagon confirms that parts have been classified to prevent the information from reaching the public.) The Pentagon dispatched Assistant Secretary of Defense for Manpower, Thomas D. Morris, to the hearings to give us what Congressman Curtis aptly terms "a report on the report." (Two days after the so-called unveiling of the Pentagon study, the President named a new citizen's commission to conduct yet another draft study. Thus, the draft issue is bounced from commission to commission, frustrating Congressional efforts at inquiry.)

It was no surprise that Morris' mission was to inform us that the long-overdue study had reached the following conclusion: The draft is necessary now and during the next decade. Morris wearily reiterated the time-worn Pentagon warnings that, without threat of the draft, voluntary enlistments would plummet, so that by the 1970's our forces would be mere skeletons of their former selves. By 1973, warned Morris, in the absence of the draft, our armed forces strength would drop to 2.2 million, 500,000 men short of the 2.7 million man force required in the ordinary peacetime years, prior to Vietnam.

Then Morris' report got down to specifics. It was true, the Pentagon conceded, that there was a way to overcome a man's traditional reluctance to enlist: raise military pay. Pay raises, they determined, could induce enough men to enlist in the armed forces to support a completely voluntary force of the 2.7 million peacetime strength. The draft could then shrivel away. But the additional cost was so fantastic, lamented the Pentagon, that the expenditure could not be justified. Then the Pentagon gave us the cost of a voluntary army with all the astonishing precision of a scattergun. The payroll increases needed to sustain an all-volunteer force of 2.7 million men, Morris reported, could range anywhere from $4 billion to $17 billion a year. The most likely figure, he said, was between $5 and $9 billion.[4] One wonders how the board of directors at Ford would have reacted if McNamara had reported: "I've nailed down production costs—give or take $4 billion." The figures were received with skepticism.

Senator Edward Kennedy said he found it "hard to believe that we cannot perform a manpower study which would indicate with more precision whether the cost of eliminating the draft would more likely be $4 billion or $20 billion, or some figure in between." (McNamara had previously stated that the cost could skyrocket to $20 billion.)

Congressman Curtis charged that the Pentagon figures were vague and meaningless, designed to create "an artificial monetary barrier to an all-volunteer army at the outset."

The Pentagon is understandably sensitive about its report of the study; for as Wool inadvertently affirmed, the figures were rigged. He said that the study had to be "revised" because the "Vietnam outlook changed it." But what did the figures reported by Morris at the House hearings have to do with Vietnam? The cost estimates in the study purported to be for a peacetime voluntary force of 2.7 million men in the 1970's presumably after the cessation of Vietnam hostilities. Morris' report did not consider the cost of a voluntary force of 3.3 million, the strength now needed for Vietnam. Why then should the basic figures in the study need to be changed in light of Vietnam? Shouldn't an estimate for a post-Vietnam *peacetime* voluntary army be the same whether it was made in 1965 or 1966?

Wool no doubt spoke the truth when he told us that the reason for "revising" the study was Vietnam. The draft is a symbol of our toughness and determination in Vietnam. The President in his 1967 State of the Union message told us that Vietnam demands "sacrifices"—a tax increase and the willingness to endure a long war. How then would it look if the Administration reported that an officially sanctioned study has forecast the end of the draft? The news could be politically embarrassing. Enlistments could drop. Hanoi and the American people might take it as a sign of "softening"—that we are planning to pull out of Vietnam. Official disapproval of the draft could open the way for more broadsides against the war itself, which is inextricably tied up in the public mind with the draft. Possibly, talk of ending the draft could have a demoralizing effect on draftees by making them realize that they are suffering because of a gross administrative oversight that did not end the draft years ago. Such Administrative rationalizing does not excuse the ruthless censorship of the Pentagon study. There will never be a time when end-the-draft proposals are not a political liability, when they do not affect the international scene. Draft proponents will always find *some* reason why we must not talk of ending the draft now. To hush up the facts during Vietnam seems particularly inexcusable, for it is during this time that the draft's inefficiency and injustices are most harmful. Congressman Curtis says: "It is criminal that successive administrations have refused to repair the leaks in the roof during sunny weather. Now the exigencies of the war are claimed to prevent real action to mend the wrongs. . . . I claim that the exigencies of the war and the continually growing demand for able manpower is an even greater reason for a review of the present system." [5]

Reluctance to release the entire study has entangled Pentagon personnel in a web of mendacity. At the University of Chicago conference, Harold Wool, as the Pentagon's representative, was pushed into hotly denying that the study was suppressed. When Congressmen Donald Rumsfield of Illinois stated that we could hardly know the "facts when the Pentagon keeps the facts secret," Wool retorted that he was "irritated by all the talk of a secret study when there is none. Everything we have has been published. It's right here," he insisted, waving the transcript of the House hearings with Morris' testimony. This testimony, incidentally, ran exactly twenty-two and a half typed pages, double-spaced, with wide margins—skimpy indeed for "the most comprehensive study of the draft ever made." Later the Pentagon supplied additional "reference" material as an appendix to the hearings transcript.[6]

In actuality, the complete uncensored study is ninety-three typed pages in text, and it has an appendix equally long. It is jammed full of charts and tables, and scattered throughout are newly inserted pages, dated March, 1966. (Presumably the revisions to which Wool referred.) Some of the conclusions directly contradict those contained in the Pentagon official release.

The suppressed study shows, what many long suspected, that the peacetime draft can be abolished, and that it is economically feasible to support a purely voluntary army at pre-Vietnam levels.

The increased cost of $4 billion to $17 billion for the voluntary army, which Morris cited, does not jibe with the findings of the suppressed report. This version places the increased cost for a voluntary army of 2.7 million men—during a time of 3 to 4 per cent unemployment—at between $4 billion and $6 billion—which, incidentally, corresponds with figures given by Walter Y. Oi, economics professor at the University of Washington. Professor Oi worked on the Pentagon study for nearly a year—from the summer of 1964 to the spring of 1965—but could not endorse the "new" conclusions of exorbitant cost and the unfeasibility of a voluntary army that were released to Congress and the American people via Morris' testimony. Oi "disagreed" with the results, he said diplomatically, and privately placed the cost of a volunteer force of 2.7 million men at $4 billion.[7]

Specifically, the secret study states that it would require "an estimated $4.2 to $6.2 billion to rely exclusively on volunteers if military strengths were to be maintained at pre-Vietnam levels." [8] Furthermore, the study suggests that the way could be paved for a voluntary army by improved army personnel policies: higher pay, greater use of civilians for nonmilitary type jobs; lower physical and mental standards, and increased fringe benefits—all the things many draft critics have been advocating for years.

The study is not optimistic about maintaining a volunteer force at current Vietnam strength of 3.3 million, and estimates the additional cost could exceed $20 billion. But the study emphatically does not support Morris' public statement which maintains that we can't get along without the draft even in peacetime. Morris' report said: "We cannot look forward to discontinuing the draft in the next decade unless changing world conditions reduce the force level substantially below those needed since Korea" [9] (below 2.7 million men). The suppressed report says just the opposite: "In the event that active duty military force requirements revert in the closing years of this decade to the levels originally planned for the current year and remain at or below this level in the early 1970's, it is possible that these measures [more pay and better personnel policies] may result in the elimination of the need for draft calls for substantial periods as we move into the 1970's. . . . It is desirable to study the implications of these trends *even at a time, such as the present,* [emphasis added] when draft calls are in fact greater than at any time in the past decade."

The Pentagon "revised" its 1965 study primarily by raising its guesses of how much military pay would have to be raised to attract the needed number of volunteers. An enlisted man now earns an average $2,500 per year for the first three years of service. First-term pay is abnormally low on the military scale because the draft provides cheap manpower for the first two and three years of service. Military pay for the "career force"—men who stay longer than three years—jumps considerably. Therefore, to induce men to enlist, first-term pay must be drastically raised. The Pentagon did not skimp; it jumped our men from peanuts to pearls. It estimated that first-term pay would have to be raised anywhere from 80 per cent to 280 per cent, depending upon the rate of unemployment (4 per cent or 5.5 per cent) and another nebulous criterion, which the Pentagon mysteriously calls its "Low, best and high" guesses.

Estimated increases in first-item pay required to obtain a 2.7 million all-volunteer force [In per cent]

	Enlisted [1]		Officers[2]
	Unemployment level		
	5.5 per cent	4.0 per cent	
Low	80	114	18
Best	111	163	26
High	181	282	50

[1] Average increase in total tax equivalent income for all enlisted men during the first 3 to 4 years of service. Tax equivalent income includes all pay and allowances plus the tax advantage resulting from the fact that quarters and subsistence allowances are not subject to income tax.

[2] Average increase in officer tax equivalent income during the first 2 years of service.

How they arrived at the figures in the chart above is not fully explained.[10] In any case, using these percentage estimates (although the Pentagon did not see fit to spell it out to Congress) we can determine what a soldier's pay over the first three years would be. The Pentagon's lowest guess is $4,500 a year. Their "best" guess, during 4 per cent unemployment, is $6,575—which would put our privates, as they rode off to boot camp, at the same salary as the average accountant. At its top estimate, the Pentagon was shameless in its determination to discourage talk of a voluntary army. It suggested starting off a private at $9,550, guaranteed for the first three years, with raises afterward—which, incidentally, is almost the median income of college presidents and deans! As Professor Oi puts it in generous understatement: "The Pentagon's high estimates are far out of line."

Only by setting all soldiers' salaries near the five-figure range was the Pentagon able to come up with its highest estimate of $17 billion for a volunteer army, which, unfortunately, is the figure most persons remember and assume to be the most probable. (When does the government spend *less* than it announces?) But in this case, the lowest estimate of $4 billion is the most realistic, and the top estimate of $17 billion is an impossible scare-figure.

Professor Oi estimates that the first-term pay for soldiers would have to be raised by 68 per cent, from $2,500 to $4,200 a year to attract the required number of volunteers for a peacetime army. So that first-term pay would not be higher than that made by soldiers in later years, Professor Oi also advises raising the pay of enlisted career men by 17 per cent. He would raise officer pay by 21 per cent. (The Pentagon would raise the pay of officers by 18 to 50 per cent.) Professor Oi, along with other statisticians who worked on the original version of the Pentagon study, concludes that the total additional cost of an all-volunteer army of peacetime strength (2.7 million men) during the 1970's would be $4 billion a year. Professor Oi emphasizes that "the cost estimates are just that, *estimates*." And that we can't *really* know the true cost until we start to put the voluntary army into operation. But since his conclusions do conform to some of the actual experiences of the smaller volunteer armies of England and Canada, Professor Oi states that he has "some confidence in these cost estimates, at least for the assumed peacetime force strength of 2.7 million men."

An additional $4 billion annually (which would increase by 33 per cent the $12 billion cost of armed forces payroll in 1965) is hardly an exorbitant price to pay for ridding ourselves of the draft and establishing more militarily effective armed forces. The extra pay for soldiers is not excessive; it is no more than they justly deserve. Professor Milton Friedman, economics professor at the University of Chicago, is a strong advocate of the voluntary army. But he urges: "We should raise soldier's pay to a living wage, regardless of any plans to move to a voluntary army."

With the Pentagon's high-cost figures demolished by their own words, there is no longer a significant financial barrier to establishing a voluntary army. But to some there are reservations, aside from cost.

The question has been raised: Could the voluntary army become a tightly knit elite corps with the power to overthrow the civilian political structure? The strong American tradition of civilian control of the military, however, has never been challenged, even in times of war, when a military takeover would be most probable. George Washington's words: "When we assumed the soldier we did not lay aside the citizen," seem to prevail.

Historically, an army of volunteers proves no more dangerous to the established social order than an army of conscripts. Napoleon came to power at the head of a conscript army, not a hand-picked professional one. So did General Francisco Franco of Spain. More recently, the 1966 military coup in Argentina was accomplished by an army composed of draftees as well as enlistees. "The point is," says Milton Friedman, "we can't say a voluntary army is any *more* of a threat to freedom than a conscript force. History shows that whether you have conscripted or voluntary forces, is irrelevant to a military takeover. The threat does not arise in any way as a result of volunteerism or compulsion."

The only danger, says Professor Friedman—and he does not find it applicable to American society—is an *insulated* officer corps, cut off from civilian life. Friedman notes in this respect that our officers are now and have always been career officers. Moreover, our standing armies in peacetime have always been purely professional armies—until nineteen years ago.

A turnover in military personnel, Professor Friedman admits, does infuse the army with civilian sentiments and prevents enlisted men from forming personal allegiances that would put army above country. Should the fear of military insulation from civilian life be a formidable obstacle to the adoption of a voluntary army, Friedman suggests the term of enlisted men could be limited to, say, five years, although this would increase the cost of the army. "I do not myself believe that the danger is sufficiently great in the U.S. to justify its adoption. But for those who do, the device offers a much better solution than continuing conscription," he says.[11]

Some persons also fear that a volunteer army would become predominantly Negro. Negroes are more frequently attracted to the armed forces because they provide psychological and material advantages not available to the poor black in civilian society. Thus, they reason, the Negro would most often be found in the recruiting lines for a voluntary army.

To be sure, the Negro re-enlistment rate is higher than that for whites, but this is based on present salaries. It is assumed that if military pay was raised, the army would attract whites also, not only the Negro disadvantaged. Additionally, Bruce Chapman, formerly an editorial writer for *The New York Herald-Tribune,* pointed out to University of Chicago conferees the impossibility of an all-Negro military: "There wouldn't be enough Negroes to fill it. Negroes tend to have a higher unfitness rejection rate than whites, but even if every single Negro male, fit or not, interested or not, upon turning eighteen—approximately 250,000 next year—were to join the Armed Forces every year, there would not be enough to meet the annual personnel turnover, even under the volunteer system." [12] It would be too bad to have to deny some Negroes the opportunity to enlist if they so wished, but if Negro over-representation proved to be a deterrent to the voluntary army, the military could easily limit the number of Negro enlistees to maintain a racial balance.

A more legitimate concern revolves around the flexibility of a voluntary army, whether it could be rapidly expanded to meet an emergency that required more men than the standing force could provide. Presumably, our Ready Reserves already exist to meet such a crisis, but few of us are so deluded as to entrust the country's fate to them, at least in their present state of pathetic unreadiness. Without a draft, it would be no longer necessary to use the Reserves as a repository for unneeded men and professional football players trying to escape the draft. The units could and should be overhauled to provide an effective back-up force.

Most importantly, a voluntary army does not preclude the reinstatement of the draft in event of a massive need for men. A voluntary army will free us of the odious presence of the draft when it is clearly not needed. In a period of total mobilization, such as World War II, when 16 million men were under arms, it would be impossible to depend solely on volunteers.

Even with a voluntary army, in the interest of national preparednes, it is probable that we would want to continue to register young men at a certain age and keep a form of Selective Service machinery dormant, as we did from 1936 to 1940—at which time, with war imminent, it was put into immediate operation. It is not my position to argue that a draft is *never* justified or that Selective Service was unsuccessful during World War II. In such a large-scale war, a truly "selective" service is probably the best mechanism for dispensing justice and meeting manpower requirements.

When not needed, the draft by definition is basically abominable and cannot be justified in a free society either morally or constitutionally. In 1918 the constitutionality of the draft law was challenged in the Supreme Court and upheld, on the basis that the Constitution gives Congress the power to raise and support armies "for the common defense." To justify the draft, the government must offer proof that conscription is essential to the defense of the country. As the American Civil Liberties Union reminds us: "The proponents of conscription always carry the burden of justifying the need for the government to force an individual to yield to compulsory military service. The justification for such invasion of civil liberties must ultimately rest upon what James Madison called 'the impulse of self-preservation.' We do not think it is inconsistent with a devotion to civil liberties for citizens to be willing to deprive themselves of some liberty in the interests of meeting a graver evil. But such deprivation of liberty, through conscription, may only be warranted by the overriding need of national security, in time of war or the imminent danger of war."

In the nineteen-year interim since the peacetime draft was initiated in 1948, the government has not assumed the burden of proving the draft essential to national survival. On the contrary, draft opponents are being forced to prove that the draft is *not* necessary. Under the Selective Service System, all men are guilty, vulnerable to bondage, until proved innocent.

It is incontrovertible that during peacetime the draft can be abolished, as admitted in the suppressed Pentagon study. Realistically, it is doubtful that the draft will be eliminated during Vietnam, even though such action may be economically feasible. (The Pentagon puts the cost of sustaining present forces of 3.3 million men at an additional $20 billion yearly. Professor Oi estimates the cost at $8 billion to $10 billion yearly.) But, surely, we should begin the "phasing out" of the draft immediately by adopting sensible military policies aimed at total abolition. During the "phasing out" period, we can accept the lottery temporarily, but we must not accept it as a *permanent* substitute. It would be disastrous, for example, to adopt the lottery without insisting on substantial pay raises for soldiers; the lottery as a lone solution could further intrench the draft.

The only conclusive way to determine the effect of changed personnel policies is to try them. What would happen if we raised military pay? If the armed forces dropped its foolish insistence that every man be fit to carry a rifle? If the military hired more civilians to fill nonmilitary jobs? If soldiers' housing was improved? If the armed forces made a *sincere* effort to recruit soldiers, and made the services more attractive for career officers, for example, doctors, instead of shuffling them in and out in two years? In short, what if we compelled the armed forces to stop using the draft as a crutch for its senseless and wasteful personnel policies?

We should find out. We should ask these questions now. We cannot let ourselves be deterred by cries that such inquiry is dangerous to national security. The Pentagon will drag out its report to prove that a voluntary army is unthinkable. Some Congressmen will call those who oppose the draft idealists, politically naïve—and worse, Vietniks. The Administration and Selective Service will attempt to shift the blame for corruption in the draft from the system, where it belongs, to those boys they call "draft-dodgers." But Americans should stand resolutely behind what John F. Kennedy called "the right to know."

They—the Selective Service, the Administration, and the Pentagon—are on trial, not we. Congress, as our representatives, should do the investigating. They should not be intimidated into petty placebo reforms that will take us into 1971 still saddled with a basically offensive draft law when the Vietnam war, we hope, will be over. Congressman Curtis believes that the President with his Advisory Commission on the draft may have effectively stalled the completion of an intensive Congressional investigation before June 30, 1967, when the law comes up for renewal. If so, there is nothing to prevent Congress from extending the authority to induct temporarily to give legislators sufficient time to make a full investigation. The very least Congress owes the American people, after two decades of needless suffering under a peacetime draft law, is a promise to end the peacetime draft as quickly as possible. That promise should be forth-coming in 1967—regardless of any other reforms in the draft. "If this is not done now," says Congressman Robert B. Kasten-meier, of Wisconsin, "it may be our last chance for freedom."

APPENDIX

Selective Service Classifications
(*In sequence*)

I-A   Available for military service.

I-A-O   Conscientious objector available for noncombatant military service only.

I-O   Conscientious objector available for civilian work contributing to the maintenance of the national health, safety, or interest.

I-S   Student deferred by statute.

I-Y   Registrant qualified for military service only in time of war or national emergency.

II-A   Registrant deferred because of civilian occupation (except agriculture and activity in study).

II-C   Registrant deferred because of agricultural occupation.

II-S   Registrant deferred because of activity in study.

I-D   Member of Reserve component or student taking military training.

III-A   Registrant with a child or children; and registrant deferred by reason of extreme hardship to dependents.

IV-B   Officials deferred by law.

IV-C   Aliens.

IV-D   Minister of religion or divinity student.

IV-F   Registrant not qualified for any military service.

IV-A   Registrant who has not completed service; sole surviving son.

V-A   Registrant over the age of liability for military service.

I-W   Conscientious objector performing civilian work contributing to the maintenance of the national health, safety, or interest.

I-C   Member of the Armed Forces of the United States, the Coast and Geodetic Survey, or the Public Health Service.

NOTES

Chapter 1. The Draft: Unquestioned

1. See Irving Werstein, *July, 1863*, New York, 1957.
2. Section 8 of the Universal Military and Service Act, as amended, states: "No person liable for training and service under this Act may furnish a substitute for that training or service. No person may be enlisted, inducted or appointed in an armed force as a substitute for another. No person liable for training and service . . . may escape that training and service or be discharged before the end of his period of training and service by paying money or any other valuable thing as a consideration for his release from that training and service or liability therefor."
3. "Is Vietnam Really a Poor Boys' War?" *U.S. News & World Report,* November 14, 1966. About 60,000 out of 331,000 U.S. military men in Vietnam were draftees at that time.
4. Review of the Administration and Operation of the Selective Service System, Hearings before the Committee on Armed Services, House of Representatives, June 22, 23, 24, 28, 29 and 30, 1966, p. 9639.
5. Robert Sherrill, "The Draft under Fire," *The Nation,* March 14, 1966.
6. Kenneth E. Boulding, "The Impact of the Draft on the Legitimacy of the National State," paper submitted to the Conference on the Draft, December 4-7, 1966, University of Chicago.

Chapter 2. The Waiting Game

1. House Armed Services Committee Hearings, op. cit., p. 9864.
2. Local Board Memorandum No. 115, March 16, 1942, cited in *Problems of Selective Service,* Special Monograph No. 16, Selective Service System, p. 143.
3. Section 5(e) of the Selective Training and Service Act of 1940 authorized the President "under such rules and regulations as he may prescribe to defer from training and service those men whose employment in industry, agriculture, or other occupations or employment, or whose activity in any other endeavor, is found . . . to be necessary to the maintenance of the national health, safety, or interest."
4. Liberty Network radio discussion, April 25, 1951, quoted by M. H. Trytten, *Student Deferment in Selective Service,* Minneapolis, 1952, p. 130.
5. Jack O'Brian, *Washington Post,* October 24, 1966. O'Brian reported that Hamilton's official biography stated that the actor was 17 in 1952 when he won "the best actor award for the state of Florida." This would make him 31 in 1966.
6. Senator Gaylord Nelson, "A Plan To End the Draft in 1967," speech in the Senate, June 29, 1964. A reprint of this speech is available from Senator Nelson's office.

Chapter 3. The Mythical Manpower Shortage

1. "Projected Manpower Needs," Hearings of the Special Subcommittee on Education of the Committee on Education and Labor, House of Representatives, February 17, 1966. These hearings were never published, but an unofficial transcript is kept in the office of the subcommittee's chairman, Congresswoman Edith Green of Oregon.

Chapter 4. The Draft Test Hoax

1. See "Wayne State University Policy on Selective Service," statement by President William R. Keast, June 16, 1966, available from his office, Wayne State University, Detroit, Michigan.
2. Norman Cousins, "Russian Roulette in the Classroom," *Saturday Review,* April 23, 1966.

3. "Draft Director Tells What's Ahead," interview with Lieutenant General Lewis B. Hershey, *U.S. News & World Report,* January 10, 1966.

4. "The Selective Service College Qualification Test Program, Spring and Summer, 1966; A Summary Report to the National Headquarters of the Selective Service System from Science Research Associates." It should be pointed out that the distribution of scores by major field is not peculiar to this test. Generally on all tests of this type, science, mathematics and humanities students score highest and education majors score lowest.

5. Ibid., p. 15, table 4.

6. Philip B. Price, M.D., et al., "Measurement of Physician Performance," *The Journal of Medical Education,* February 1964, p. 203.

7. Eli Ginzberg and John L. Herma, *Talent and Performance,* New York, 1964, pp. 89-111.

Chapter 5. Privileged Not To Serve

1. House Armed Services Committee Hearings, op. cit., p. 9721.

2. Ibid., p. 10011.

3. Walter Y. Oi, "The Costs and Implications of an All-Volunteer Force," paper presented to the Conference on the Draft, December 4-7, 1966, University of Chicago, p. 59.

4. House Armed Services Committee Hearings, op. cit., p. 10012.

5. John Frook, "The Wizard of Flunk-Out U," *Life,* June 3, 1966.

6. Congressional Record, Proceedings and Debates of the 76th Congress, 3rd Session, September 6, 1940, pp. 11655-11656.

7. Ibid, September 7, 1940, p. 11705.

8. Richard de Neufville and Caryl Conner, "How Good Are Our Schools?" *American Education,* October 1966.

Chapter 6. Local Boards: An Anachronism

1. Report of Availability and Summary of Classification, November 30, 1966, Selective Service System.

2. House Armed Services Committee Hearings, op. cit., p. 9912.

3. Ibid., p. 9698.

4. "An Equal Draft Obligation on Each State," Press Release, June 1, 1966, issued from the office of Senator Robert P. Griffin,

Michigan. The Wednesday Club issued a series of six releases on the draft, each criticizing a separate phase.

5. House Armed Services Committee Hearings, op. cit., p. 9763.
6. Ibid., p. 9764.
7. Roger W. Little, "Selective Service in Illinois," paper presented at the National Conference on the Draft, American Veterans Committee, Washington, D. C., November 11-12, 1966.

Chapter 7. General Hershey: Master Planner

1. House Armed Services Committee Hearings, op. cit., p. 9622.
2. Congressional Record, House, July 28, 1966, p. 16761.
3. Quoted in *The Manpower Revolution; Its Policy Consequences,* Excerpts from the Senate Hearings Before the Clark Subcommittee, edited by Garth L. Mangum, New York, 1965, p. 251.
4. See "Review of Military Manpower Procurement System Based on the Draft," a reprint of the speeches of 16 Republican Congressmen who made a full-scale attack on the draft in the House on April 21, 1964. Reprint is available from the office of Congressman Thomas Curtis, Missouri.

Chapter 8. Persecution of Dissenters

1. Congressional Record-Appendix, April 28, 1966, p. A2324.
2. *Wolff, et al. v. Selective Service Local Board No. 16, et al.,* February 2, 1967, Second Circuit, Docket No. 30783, decided January 30, 1967.
3. John Reints, Memorandum, September 1966, to the Executive Board of the Central Committee for Conscientious Objectors.
4. Richard E. Rubenstein, "We're Unfair to Draft-Card Burners," *Saturday Evening Post,* February 12, 1966.
5. Quoted by Chandler Brossard, "Draft Resisters 1965," *Look,* December 28, 1965.

Chapter 9. The Military Accomplice

1. Roscoe S. Conkling, *The Case Against Compulsory Military Training,* New York, Post War World Council, 1945.
2. John M. Swomley, Jr., *The Military Establishment,* Boston, 1964, pp. 53-66.
3. Annual Report of the Director of Selective Service, 1965.

4. Hearings, Subcommittee on Employment and Manpower Senate Committee on Labor and Public Welfare, November 12, 1963, Pt. 8, pp. 2592-2595.
5. Technical Research Report 1132, Development of Armed Forces Qualification Test 7 and 8, U.S. Army Personnel Research Office, Washington, D.C.
6. Congressional Record, House, June 25, 1964.
7. Swomley, op. cit., pp. 45-80.
8. Congressional Record, August 25, 1965, p. 20911.
9. "Review of Military Manpower Procurement System Based on the Draft," op. cit.

Chapter 10. Proposals for Reform

1. Kenneth Boulding, "The Impact of the Draft on the Legitimacy of the National State," op. cit.
2. House Armed Services Committee Hearings, op. cit., p. 9843.
3. Ibid., p. 10067.
4. Margaret Mead, "A National Service System as a Solution to a Variety of National Problems," paper presented to the Conference on the Draft, December 4-7, 1966, at the University of Chicago.
5. Dwight D. Eisenhower, "This Country *Needs* Universal Military Training," *Reader's Digest,* September, 1966.

Chapter 11. The Case for Abolishing the Draft

1. Senator Gaylord Nelson, Congressional Record, February 9, 1965.
2. Defense Advisory Committee on Professional and Technical Compensation, "A Modern Concept of Compensation for Personnel of the Uniformed Services," March, 1957.
3. "The Lost Report," *The Nation,* February 7, 1966.
4. House Armed Services Committee Hearings, op. cit., p. 9939.
5. Congressman Thomas B. Curtis, speech in the House, April 20, 1966.
6. House Armed Services Committee Hearings, op. cit., pp. 9999-10052.
7. Walter Y. Oi, "The Costs and Implications of an All-Volunteer Force," op. cit., p. 45.

8. Department of Defense, "Meeting Our Military Manpower Requirements," March 4, 1966. Unpublished. The quotations are from notes I made during my unauthorized reading of the study. It is not possible to cite page numbers, for some pages were unnumbered, and the sequence was broken up by the insertion of new pages for the 1966 "revision."

9. House Armed Services Committee Hearings, op. cit., p. 9942.

10. Ibid., p. 9958.

11. Professor Milton Friedman, "Why Not a Voluntary Army?", paper submitted to the Conference on the Draft, December 4-7, 1966, University of Chicago.

12. Bruce K. Chapman, "Politics and Conscription: A Proposal to Replace the Draft," a paper presented to the Conference on the Draft, December 4-7, 1966, University of Chicago.

INDEX

Franco, Gen. Francisco, 186
Friedenberg, Dr. Edgar Z., 143
Friedman, Milton, 186–187
Frost, Robert, 82
Ft. Polk, Mississippi, 144
Ft. Sam Houston, Mississippi, 144

Galbraith, John Kenneth, 176
Gallup poll, 15, 163
General Electric, 177
General Motors Corporation, 99
George Washington University, 121
Georgia, 24, 41, 107
Gettysburg, Pennsylvania, 13
Ginzberg, Eli, 79
Glenn, John, 82
Goldwater, Barry, 175
Goodman, Paul, 39, 65, 87
Graham, Sheilah, 42
Gray, Dorian, 15
Gray, Col. Samuel F., 149
Greece, 152
Greeley, Horace, 12
Green, Mrs. Edith, 78, 107
Gross, Brig. Gen. Henry M., 124
Growing Up Absurd, 39
Gruening, Ernest, 21
Guadalcanal, 75

Halpern, Seymour, 33
Hamilton, Bill, 42
Hamilton, Dave, 42
Hamilton, George, 42–43, 147, 165
Hammack, John H., 109
Hanalian, Leo, 64
Hanoi, 181
Harrison, Paul M., 74
Hart, Philip A., 131
The Harvard Crimson, 33, 88
Harvard University, 65, 74, 77, 85, 88–89, 170, 176
Hay, John, 64
Hazard, Geoffrey C., Jr., 83, 164
Hemingway, Ernest, 78, 82
Hershey, Lt. Gen. Lewis Blaine, 17–19, 22–24, 31–32, 34, 36–37, 39–44, 46–51, 53–61, 63, 66–

68, 70–72, 75–76, 80, 82–84, 86–87, 91–92, 95–99, 101–109, 111–117, 119–135, 137, 139–140, 143, 145, 147, 149–152, 159, 161, 163–167, 169, 175, 178
Hershey Chocolate Company, 111
Hitler, Adolf, 76, 141, 171
Holifield, Chet, 105, 109
Holmes, Col. Arthur, 129–130, 134
Honolulu, Hawaii, 65
Hoover, J. Edgar, 17
House Armed Services Committee, 17, 22, 24–25, 44, 56–57, 71, 82, 87, 97–98, 102, 105, 109, 113, 120, 163, 166, 179–180, 182
House Committee on Education and Labor, 49, 60, 67, 78, 132
House of Representatives, U.S., 59, 88, 127, 155, 167, 178
Housman, A. E., 79–80
Hutchins, Robert, 136

Idaho, 149
Illinois, 50, 90, 101, 109, 130, 133, 182
Illinois, University of, 109
Indiana, 17, 68
Indiana National Guard, 111
Ingold, Col. Dee, 58, 70, 83–84
Internal Revenue Service, 99
IBM, 19, 99
Iowa, 136
Italy, 152

James, William, 170
Janowitz, Morris, 73, 168, 171
Javits, Jacob K., 97, 170
John XXIII, 142
Johnson, Lyndon B., 19–20, 42n, 46, 151, 157, 160, 175, 178–179, 181, 190
Joint Center for Urban Studies of MIT and Harvard, 27
Jolliff, James, 144
Justice Department, U.S., 136, 138

Kansas, 68, 125